DECISION ON THE

*H*udson

THE BATTLES OF SARATOGA

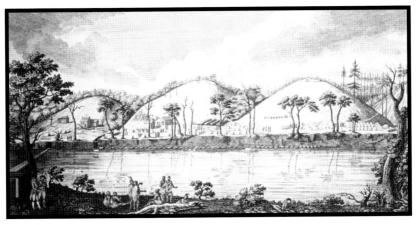

The Great Redoubt

Written by: John Luzader

Saratoga National Historical Park
New York

Published by: Eastern National, www.eParks.com

Eastern National provides quality educational products and services to
America's national parks and other public trusts.

ISBN 1-888213-59-0

Design: Mo Martin, Martin/Cannata Graphics
♻ Printed on recycled paper

Originally published 1975, Office of Publications,
National Park Service, U.S. Department of the Interior
Revised and reprinted 2002 by Eastern National

Acknowledgments:
National Park Service employees are asked to undertake an ever-increasing
variety of tasks often in addition to their normal work assignments. That is
why the assistance that they provided with this re-publication effort is so
appreciated. Eric Schnitzer researched and updated the text and prepared the
battle maps, as well as some illustrations. Duncan Morrow provided editorial
suggestions for much of the text. Thanks also to park staff members Richard
Beresford, Joseph Craig, Rebecca Hammell, Gina Johnson, and William Valosin
who helped with research and writing. Recognition also goes to Hunt Conard
of Skidmore College for his special assistance with graphic imaging. Finally,
thanks go to Eastern National for their support and financial assistance to
produce this revised text.

Cover image: The Battle at Barber's Wheatfield, October 7, 1777.
Illustration by Don Troiani, Saratoga National Historical Park

Title page: The Great Redoubt. Courtesy Anne S. K. Brown Military Collection,
Brown University Library

Table of Contents

Preface

ecision on the Hudson, the handbook for Saratoga National Historical Park, was originally published in 1975 and was written by Park Historian John Luzader. Now, after not being available for some years, *Decision on the Hudson* is back in print, and with a new look. The most obvious difference is the selection of a new set of images that have completely replaced the original ones. We now present you with a larger variety of illustrations, many of which are contemporary images from the period. Readers will also benefit from the inclusion of new maps, many of which are based on drawings done during the war.

The text has been edited and supplemented as well. The campaign is still presented primarily from the British point of view, but more light is put on the American side of the story. Also, groups of people and individuals whose accounts have previously not been told are now properly introduced. As new and more refined accounts of the events of 1777 have come to light, they have helped to give life and form to these momentous events. These first-person accounts, as well as some new scholarship, have been utilized to bring this history of the campaign of 1777 up-to-date and make it as vivid as possible.

Foreword

For the rebelling Americans the year 1776 held many highs and lows. While the adoption of the Declaration of Independence had filled many with the hope of establishing a new nation, they found that proclaiming independence was one matter, winning it was proving much more difficult.

During the summer, British General William Howe had invaded Long Island and lower New York. His professional troops outmaneuvered and defeated General George Washington's ill-trained forces defending the city. Foul weather and desertion further beset the ragged Continental Army, but fortunately for the cause of Independence, Howe's troops could never decisively trap or defeat Washington. Still, the revolutionary army's condition after retreating across New Jersey into Pennsylvania hardly inspired much confidence.

The Americans' situation to the north was not much better. Their invasion of British-held Canada deteriorated from an unsuccessful siege of Québec to a disorderly retreat. Plagued by smallpox and hounded by a reinforced Royal Army, the surviving troops devolved into little more than an ill-disciplined mob fleeing south, barely able to hang onto the forts at Crown Point, Ticonderoga, and Mount Independence. The Americans' control of strategic Lake Champlain hung in the balance. To counter the anticipated British naval offensive, the Americans under Benedict Arnold feverishly built gunboats and trained their crews. The fleets clashed in mid-October, but despite putting up a fierce fight, the American naval force was lost, together with its valuable arms and supplies.

As 1776 ended, the struggle for American Independence seemed all but over. While Washington's successful gambles at the Battles of Trenton and Princeton kept hopes alive, the British still held the initiative. Royal garrisons held Canada, lower New York, Long Island, and Newport, Rhode Island, and the unopposed Royal Navy enabled the British to strike at will up and down the eastern seaboard.

Not only were critical water transportation routes under British control, but the Americans also suffered debilitating shortages of food, supplies, and munitions. Native manufacturing could not realistically supply the army's needs. Although individual states could tax, the Continental Congress relied on contributions to finance its troops and their munitions and supplies. France had provided some unofficial support, but to continue the cause, significant military help in the form of naval forces, arms, and money was desperately needed.

With defeat looming large, the 1777 campaign opened. The survival—perhaps even the arrival—of a truly free and independent United States of America was very much in doubt. The north appeared ripe for British conquest, but the Americans were not yet ready for surrender.

A Note to the Reader

In the 18th century, spelling and grammar were often phonetic and varied, allowing for some very creatively written documents.

In the following text, words or sentences that are in quotes or are marginal and italicized are the original words used by the writer when written in the 18th century. There has been no attempt to standardize spelling or punctuation. At times, an occasional word between brackets will be found in the text. The word in the brackets is not original to the 18th-century version, but has been added to help define a word, or correct a gross error.

Throughout the following text, the ranks of the individuals involved in the American War for Independence are given. When first mentioned, the individual's full name and rank are printed, as in "Major General Horatio Gates." Subsequently, a simplified "General Gates" or "Gates" is used. Below is a list, from highest to lowest, of different ranks used in an 18th-century army, which is very similar to the ranking system of today:

GENERAL

LIEUTENANT GENERAL

MAJOR GENERAL

BRIGADIER GENERAL (OR BRIGADIER)

COLONEL

LIEUTENANT COLONEL

MAJOR

CAPTAIN

CAPTAIN LIEUTENANT

LIEUTENANT (OR 1ST LIEUTENANT)

ENSIGN (OR 2ND LIEUTENANT)

SERGEANT MAJOR

SERGEANT

CORPORAL

PRIVATE

1777: Year of Decision

ort St. Jean, Québec, was no stranger to war and soldiers. Situated on the Richelieu River near the staging area between Lake Champlain and the St. Lawrence River, it occupied an important site on an old invasion route between Canada and New York. Successful and defeated soldiers had marched past, and rebellious Americans had captured it twice during the first year of the Revolutionary War. During the early days of June 1777, it witnessed the opening of still another chapter in history as Lieutenant General John Burgoyne's army assembled there to launch a new British offensive along Lake Champlain, Lake George, and the Hudson River.

General John Burgoyne

The commander of the army and author of the plan for the campaign, 55-year-old John Burgoyne, was scion of an old Lancashire family and a man of many talents: veteran of 30 years' military service, member of Parliament, and playwright. He was, in many ways, a representative of the upper-class county families who dominated the political, social, and military life of 18th-century England. Intelligent, handsome, and humane, he was popular with his troops, who gave him the sobriquet "Gentleman Johnny." His less attractive traits were vanity and excessive ambition.

General Burgoyne's American service began on May 25, 1775, when he and Major Generals William Howe and Henry Clinton arrived in Boston to serve under Lieutenant General Thomas Gage, whose troops were then under siege by rebel forces. That tour of duty was brief and ended when he returned to England the next November. Burgoyne's service in Boston was undistinguished, but in a memorandum to General Gage he set forth his views on the importance of the region with which his future career was to be so closely associated:

> *I have always thought Hudson's River the most proper*
> *part of the whole continent for opening vigorous operations.*
> *Because the course of the river, so beneficial for conveying*

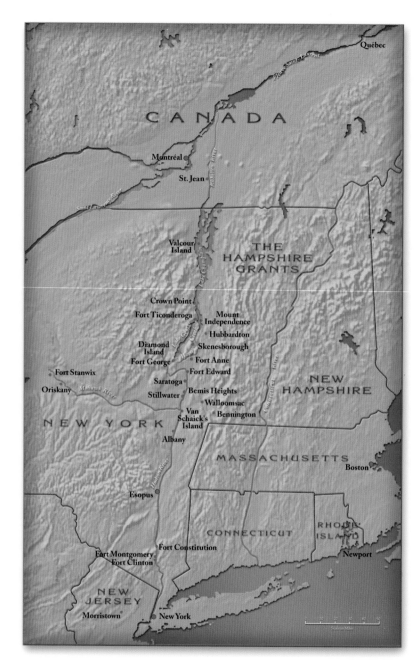

The Northern Campaign of 1777

MAP BY DAVID CURRAN, SARATOGA NATIONAL HISTORICAL PARK

DECISION ON THE HUDSON

all the bulky necessaries of an army, is precisely the route that an army ought to take for the great purposes of cutting the communications between the Southern and Northern Provinces, giving confidence to the Indians, and securing a junction with the Canadian forces. These purposes effected, and a fleet upon the coast, it is to me morally certain that the forces of New England must be reduced so early in the campaign to give you battle upon your terms, or perish before the end of it for want of necessary supplies.

Burgoyne was not the first to appreciate the strategic significance of the Lake Champlain-Lake George-Hudson River waterway. It had been a military route since pre-colonial times. Algonquian and Iroquois Indians used it during the generations of trade and warfare for the domination of the Old Northwest. French, Dutch, and English soldiers used it during their struggles for colonial empire. For nearly a century before the American Revolution, the tides of war had ebbed and flowed along this route, and Forts St. Jean, St. Frederick, Crown Point, Ticonderoga, William Henry, George, Anne, Edward, Miller, and Hardy had been built to exploit and secure its military potential. For traders, missionaries, and settlers, it was a highway linking Canada and the City of New York.

Burgoyne's belief in the strategic importance of the historic route was shared by both British and American strategists. In 1775, the Americans' abortive Canadian campaign, undertaken to add that Province to the roster of rebellious colonies, reflected an appreciation of the region's military and political importance. The resultant British counteroffensive in 1776 under General Sir Guy Carleton was based upon the same strategic assessment.

Carleton, governor and commanding general in Canada, began his campaign by driving the Americans back into New York. Then, in June 1776, he launched his army south on the Champlain-Hudson route toward Albany. From there he planned to cooperate with forces under General William

General Sir Guy Carlton

(1724-1808) WAS THE GOVERNOR WHO SUCCESS- FULLY DEFENDED CANADA FOR BRITAIN IN 1775-6. THE PERSONAL ANIMOSITY OF THE BRITISH COLONIAL SECRETARY, LORD GERMAIN, WAS ONE OF THE REASONS FOR BURGOYNE BEING CHOSEN TO LEAD THE 1777 OFFENSIVE FROM CANADA.

COURTESY FORT TICONDEROGA MUSEUM

Lord George Germain

Howe advancing northward from the City of New York. The British would then dominate upper New York; communications between the City of New York and Canada would be secured, and New England, the heart of the rebellion, would be caught between the sea and a successful, united Royal Army. These goals were not realized because Howe's advance ended on the Delaware River instead of the upper Hudson. The hasty construction of an American flotilla under Brigadier General Benedict Arnold and the subsequent battle off Valcour Island on Lake Champlain damaged and helped to delay Carleton's victorious forces. With winter approaching, the British commander decided to retire his army to Canada.

Burgoyne was disappointed by his role in Carleton's 1776 offensive. He had hoped for an independent field command and conditions had favored his chances. Lord George Germain, colonial secretary and the minister responsible for the conduct of the war in America, was determined that Carleton should not command the advance from Canada. His first choice was General Henry Clinton, but Clinton had been ordered south on what turned out to be an unsuccessful expedition against Charleston, South Carolina, and was not available. It seemed that Burgoyne's hour had arrived: he was dispatched to Canada as Carleton's second-in-command and commissioned to lead the offensive. Storms delayed delivery of the letter assigning him the field command, and when Burgoyne arrived, Carleton had already begun operations. Lacking orders to relinquish his command to his subordinate, Carleton retained it, and Burgoyne functioned as his second-in-command. Carleton's failure to pass Lake Champlain and secure the upper Hudson did not enhance his reputation at court.

Like Clinton and some other officers who were members of Parliament, Burgoyne returned to England at the end of 1776 to attend the winter sessions and to advance his personal interests. He carried a letter from Carleton recommending him to the colonial secretary as a source of information and advice.

General Sir William Howe

(1729-1814) BRITISH
COMMANDER–IN–CHIEF IN
NORTH AMERICA 1776-78. HIS
OPERATIONS IN 1777 AGAINST
GENERAL GEORGE WASHING–
TON'S ARMY IN THE AREA OF
PHILADELPHIA ARE SOMETIMES
VIEWED AS CONTRIBUTIONS TO
THE DEFEAT OF GENERAL BUR–
GOYNE'S FORCES AT SARATOGA.

Burgoyne used this to his own advantage, openly soliciting command of the next northern offensive.

The man who held the key to his appointment was 61-year-old Lord George Germain. Son of the First Duke of Dorset, Germain had started military life as a captain in the British army, and he eventually rose to the rank of major general. That career had ended in 1760 when a court-martial found him guilty of disobeying orders during the Battle of Minden the year before. He was dismissed from the army and deemed "unfit to serve…in any military capacity whatever." A member of Parliament since 1746, Germain concentrated on a political career and made the slow, difficult ascent to influence, eventually becoming a supporter of Lord Frederick North, who became Prime Minister in March 1770. Although he lacked a personal following in the House of Commons and had a number of personal and political enemies, Germain became colonial secretary on November 10, 1775.

Advocating a staunch, coercive policy against the rebellious Americans, Germain energetically mobilized Britain's resources for the prosecution of the war. Thousands of troops were raised, trained, equipped, and transported to North America. His responsibilities were not limited to allocating resources however; they also included the development and definition of Britain's grand strategy. This involved cooperative relations with the two commanders he inherited when he came to office: William Howe and Guy Carleton.

Germain's relations with Howe during 1776 had been amicable, but his attitude toward Carleton was very different. A hostility of obscure origin existed between them. That fed every opportunity for friction until it ripened into a hatred that both men nurtured.

The Carleton-Germain feud bore fruit that poisoned British military administration in America. When General Gage was recalled to England in October 1775, Carleton became the senior general officer in North America—status that normally would have guaranteed him the command of the united British army whenever the forces from Canada and those from the Atlantic seaboard should merge. But Germain's hostility blocked the general's chances of ever realizing this prospect. Instead of providing for an eventual unified command, the government kept the forces in North America divided into two independent armies. General Howe became commander-in-chief in the "thirteen colonies," replacing Gage, while Carleton retained the Canadian command. Germain's determination that Carleton should not lead an offensive from Canada was consistent with this division of authority.

Ministers at Whitehall in Britain assumed that the Champlain-Hudson offensive would be resumed in 1777. The most obvious question was who would lead it. With Carleton eliminated, the choice lay between Burgoyne and Henry Clinton, Howe's second-in-command, who, like Burgoyne, was unhappy in his subordinate status. Both men were in London and both were eager for independent commands. Clinton was the senior of the two and he could have had the assignment had he asked for it. But he did not solicit the command, probably because he believed that Howe would give it to him when the army from Canada came under that general's authority. After considering

A VIEW OF FORT TICONDEROGA
FROM A POINT ON THE NORTH SHORE
OF LAKE CHAMPLAIN, 1777.

JAMES HUNTER/
NATIONAL ARCHIVES OF CANADA/ C-001524

Clinton, the Cabinet decided to send Burgoyne back to Canada to lead the next offensive. Clinton received a knighthood and returned to New York as Howe's second-in-command, in a position to succeed the commander-in-chief should he resign or become incapacitated.

Burgoyne was not idle while his professional future was being considered. He was busy preparing proposals for the next northern campaign. On February 28, 1777, he sent Germain his *Thoughts for Conducting the War from the Side of Canada.*

The first objective of the campaign would be to secure the navigation of Lake Champlain. Crown Point would then be captured and used as a temporary base of operations. Fort Ticonderoga, the first major obstacle to the advance southward, would fall early in the summer, when it would "then become a more proper place for arms than Crown Point." Once these fortified places were secured, "The next measure must depend upon those taken by the enemy, and upon the general plan of the campaign as concerted at home." If the ministry decided that General Howe's entire army would act on the Hudson and "if the only object of the Canada army is to effect a junction with that force," Burgoyne proposed to advance to Albany by way of Lake George. Otherwise, he suggested that his army might cooperate with troops in Rhode Island to gain control of the Connecticut River, stating that "Should the junction between the Canada and Rhode Island armies be effected upon the Connecticut, it would not be too sanguine an expectation that all the New England provinces will be reduced by their operations." Burgoyne also believed that a secondary offensive by way of Lake Ontario and the Mohawk River would be desirable "as a diversion to facilitate every proposed operation." Should these propositions be considered impractical and the force from Canada too small to undertake an overland campaign, it might be wise to transfer it by sea to join Howe in New York. Nothing in Burgoyne's proposals suggested that garrisoning the Champlain-George-Hudson line and isolating New England were the objectives of the campaign. British success on the Hudson might result in a strategic isolation of New England, but the general did not develop this thesis in his *Thoughts for Conducting the War from the Side of Canada.*

Because his proposals were, in the final analysis, a discussion of alternatives, Burgoyne did not precisely define his objectives. As he noted in connection with proposed moves following the reduction of Ticonderoga, his course would depend "upon the general plan of the campaign as concerted at home." He assumed that King George III and his ministers would draft a comprehensive plan for 1777 defining how he and General Howe would coordinate their activities. In only one instance, and that somewhat ambiguous, did Burgoyne anticipate what his objective might be: "These ideas are formed upon the supposition that it be the sole purpose of the Canadian army to effect a junction with General Howe, or after cooperating so far as to get possession of Albany and open the communication to New York, to remain upon the Hudson's River, and thereby enable that general to act with his whole force to the southward." He thus expected that the two generals would act in concert, but he did not detail how or to what extent this should be done.

While Burgoyne worked out his proposals for 1777, General Howe was developing his own ideas, and during the course of several months he drafted plans that were to have significant repercussions on the outcome of the campaign. Like Carleton, Howe had served in America during The French and Indian War, commanding the 58th Regiment of Foot in General Jeffrey Amherst's successful operation against Louisbourg, Nova Scotia, in 1758.

George III, King of Great Britain and Ireland

The next year he headed the light infantry battalion that led General James Wolfe's force onto the Heights of Abraham in the capture of Québec City. He also commanded a "brigade of detachments" in 1760, when Amherst captured Montréal. A Whig member of Parliament from Nottingham and a critic of the ministry's repressive American policies, he nevertheless returned to America with Clinton and Burgoyne in May 1775 to serve under General Gage in Boston. He personally commanded the British troops in the Battle of Bunker Hill on June 17 and later succeeded Gage as commander-in-chief.

After evacuating Boston in March 1776, Howe more than redeemed the British position in America during the following summer and autumn. At Long Island, NY, on August 27, he soundly defeated General George Washington's Continental Army in the "first pitched battle" of the war. He followed this success by capturing the City of New York and Forts Washington and Lee on the Hudson; but he failed to profit by his tactical advantage, and Washington escaped across New Jersey with most of his army. The American general's retreat to Pennsylvania surprised the British who had expected him to take refuge in New England. By pursuing Washington, Howe ended his campaign on the Delaware, making it impossible for him to cooperate with Carleton on the Hudson.

While Howe displayed sound strategic and tactical skill, he had not been very aggressive in following up his advantages. Nevertheless, he retained the king's and Germain's favor and was knighted for his victory on Long Island.

On November 30, 1776, while Washington's demoralized army retreated across New Jersey, Sir William Howe wrote two letters to Germain. In the first he reported on the successful operations around the City of New York. In the second he informed the colonial secretary that he intended to quarter a large body of troops in East Jersey for the winter and that he expected the Americans would try to cover their capital, Philadelphia, by establishing a line on either the Raritan or Delaware Rivers. Howe also notified Germain that Carleton had abandoned his offensive upon Lake Champlain. He presumed that it would be renewed in the spring, but he did not expect the Canadian army to reach Albany until September. Carleton's performance made this a reasonable assumption. Upon this premise, Howe proposed a plan he believed might "finish the War in one Year by an extensive and vigorous Exertion of His Majesty's arms."

His plan was essentially a continuation of current strategy against New England. Briefly stated, he proposed two simultaneous offensives: one, with Rhode Island as a base, to be directed at Boston; the second to move north along the Hudson and rendezvous with the renewed advance from Canada. A third force would act in New Jersey to check Washington by exploiting the American fears for the safety of Philadelphia, which Howe "proposed to attack in the Autumn, as well as Virginia, provided the Success of the operations will admit of an adequate Force to be sent against that Province." South Carolina and Georgia would be the objectives of a winter campaign. This ambitious plan would require two additional ships of the line and at least 35,000 men. Placing his present strength at 20,000, Howe figured that he needed a reinforcement of 15,000 men. He knew that these could not be raised in Great Britain and suggested that the government hire troops from Russia and several German states.

On December 20, ten days before his letters of November 30 reached London, Howe wrote another letter to Germain containing a new plan. At that time, the British seemed to have firm control of New Jersey, and Howe believed that American capabilities to continue the fight were diminishing. He also thought the sentiments of the Pennsylvanians were turning toward peace, "in which Sentiment they would be confirmed by our getting Possession of Philadelphia." He was "fully persuaded the Principal Army should act offensively on that side." This change in priorities required that the New England offensive be postponed until after reinforcements arrived from Europe, so that "there might be a Corps to act defensively on the lower part of Hudson's River to cover Jersey and to facilitate in some degree the approach of the Canada Army." Howe lowered his troop requirements from 35,000 to 19,000, which he proposed to distribute in the following manner: 2,000 in Rhode Island, 4,000 in the City of New York, 3,000 to operate on the lower Hudson, and 10,000 for the campaign against Philadelphia.

Howe's second plan represented a major change in strategy. Concerted operations against New England would be abandoned in favor of a campaign in Pennsylvania, and the renewed Champlain-Hudson offensive would have to be undertaken without a comparable effort on the lower part of the river. The lowering of manpower requirements was a retreat from the need to meet immediate short-range objectives.

Before either of Howe's plans could be received in London, the situation in New Jersey took a dramatic turn that dissipated his fragile optimism and decisively affected his thinking. With an audacity born of desperation, Washington attacked and captured most of Howe's German Hessian troops at Trenton on the morning of December 26. He then defeated a British force at Princeton and executed a skillful withdrawal into the hills around Morristown. Washington's army, which had teetered on the brink of dissolution, did not merely continue to exist—it regained West Jersey.

Howe's November 30 correspondence containing his first plan reached London on December 30. In a letter dated February 14, 1777, Germain told Howe that the king would "defer sending you his Sentiments on your Plan for the next Campaign until He was enabled to take the whole into His Royal Consideration." On February 23, Germain received the December 20 letter containing Howe's second plan, as well as a dispatch dated December 29 reporting on the Battles of Trenton and Princeton. The colonial secretary's reply to Howe on March 3 approved the plan to attack Philadelphia in these words: "I am now commanded to acquaint you that the King entirely approves of your proposed Deviation from the Plan which you formerly suggested, being of Opinion that the Reasons which have induced you to recommend this change in your Operations are solid and decisive."

While the government in London studied Burgoyne's and Howe's proposals and prepared its own plans for 1777, Howe became increasingly pessimistic. He believed that the winning of the war required the steady expansion of the British occupation as well as the destruction of the American army. Frustrated by the government's inability to provide him with adequate reinforcements and by his own failure to bring Washington to battle on British terms, he decided to alter his plans for the attack on Philadelphia. Washington's position on Howe's flank ruled out a direct advance across New Jersey, and crossing the Delaware with 90 miles of exposed communications in his rear would be folly. On April 2 Howe sent a third plan to Germain in which he proposed to abandon the overland route to Philadelphia in favor of one by sea. His letter contained a revealing note: "Restricted as I am, from entering upon more extensive operations by the want of force, my hopes of terminating the war this year are vanished." But he expected by the end of the campaign to hold New York, Pennsylvania, and New Jersey, "though that must depend upon the success of the Northern Army."

The change from a land to a sea route had important results. First, it delayed the opening of the campaign. Secondly, it removed Howe's army from between Washington and both Clinton and Burgoyne. Washington could not abandon the defense of Philadelphia, but he could send troops northward to help check the advance from Canada. Thirdly, by taking the major part of his army to sea, Howe made it impossible for him either to cooperate with Burgoyne or to go to his assistance should he get into difficulty. The force of 3,900 regulars and 3,000 loyalists that Howe left in New York under Sir Henry Clinton was too small to carry out either of those contingencies. The British had thus lost the degree of tactical flexibility they needed to cope with the two main American armies in the north that were potentially numerically superior, relatively mobile, and operating on interior lines.

Behind Howe's second and third plans lay three important attitudes. In the first place, he did not believe that the Americans could prevent Burgoyne from reaching Albany. Secondly, he believed that his obligation to cooperate was not concerned with helping Burgoyne reach Albany, but rather to help maintain him once he arrived there. And thirdly, as had been the case with Carleton's campaign in 1776, Howe, while paying lip-service to the importance of the invasion from Canada, demonstrated little interest in it.

Sir William Howe and John Burgoyne could draft proposals and plans, but the king and his ministers were responsible for making the final decisions. They selected from among the available alternatives and tried to coordinate the efforts of the armies in the field, to define objectives, to assign priorities, and to apportion resources. The minister most intimately involved in this process was Colonial Secretary Germain. At the time he and his colleagues began developing their plans for 1777 they were still ignorant of the dramatic and fateful events of Trenton and Princeton, and they could look back on 1776 with some satisfaction. Large armies had been raised, equipped, and transported to North America; Canada was still British; the City of New York and Long Island were reclaimed; and as far as anyone in London knew, New Jersey was securely in British hands. The rebellion seemed almost crushed.

While the king and the ministry had reason to congratulate themselves, the failure to win the American war by the close of 1776 exposed Britain to dangers that only a victory in 1777 could dispel. The concentration of so much of her military capability in America was a bold, calculated gamble taken in the face of a possible French attack. They weighed this danger against the greater advantage of ending the rebellion before European neighbors could intervene to Britain's detriment.

That the rebellion was almost crushed was not enough. Its total defeat had to be accomplished as soon as possible. During the summer of 1776 France had inched toward war, convinced that she faced an opportunity to redeem the interests and prestige she had lost in the Seven Years' War (in America, it is also called The French and Indian War, 1754-1763). The French were already "unofficially" providing munitions and other military supplies to the Americans. The decision to openly join the rebellion would depend upon events in America. Would Britain and the Colonies be reconciled? Could the Americans continue to fight with reasonable hopes for making independence a reality? British successes on Long Island and Manhattan seemed to answer in the negative, and France drew back. The amazing American recovery that attended and followed Trenton and Princeton made it even more obvious that England needed an early, decisive victory to make French neutrality permanent.

When George III and his ministers studied Burgoyne's proposals, they had at hand Howe's first plan for 1777; his letter of December 20 altering that plan by shifting the offensive priority from New England to Philadelphia (to which the king gave his assent on March 3); and Howe's letter of December 29 reporting the American successes at Trenton and Princeton. The British leaders accepted the broad outline of Burgoyne's proposals and directed him to "force his way to Albany," supported by a diversion moving east down the Mohawk Valley under the command of Lieutenant Colonel Barry St. Leger. Burgoyne and St. Leger would meet at Albany and put themselves under Sir William Howe's command. Pending receipt of orders from Howe, Burgoyne was to act as his judgment and tactical situation required, always remembering that his main objective was a junction with his new commander. Howe was not required to meet Burgoyne and St. Leger at Albany, and Burgoyne, in defining the campaign's purpose, had not insisted upon a physical rendezvous. He would join Howe or cooperate with him in a way that would facilitate the latter's southern operations. In short, everyone, including Burgoyne himself, expected the army from Canada to reach Albany without assistance from the south.

As noted earlier, Germain's March 3 letter to Howe approved the plan to attack Philadelphia. Howe's letter of April 2 proposing to take his army to Pennsylvania by sea was not received until May 8, after the other elements of the plans had been approved and after Burgoyne had returned to Canada. Ten days later, Germain wrote that the king, confident of Howe's judgment, approved of any alteration in plan that the general thought wise, "trusting, however, that whatever you may mediate, it will be executed in time for you to cooperate with the army ordered to proceed from Canada and put itself under your command." Because a letter dispatched in mid-May could not reach Howe for several weeks, the king and his colonial secretary had no choice but to concur. Their response was promptly posted, but it did not reach Howe until he was on the Chesapeake Bay en route to Philadelphia. By that time the only part of Howe's army that could cooperate with Burgoyne was that portion left in and around the City of New York under Sir Henry Clinton. Clinton had received no positive orders, nor did he have enough men, to go to Burgoyne's relief should that army encounter more opposition than expected and need assistance.

Invasion

urgoyne returned to Canada on May 6. On June 13, in a solemn ceremony at St. Jean, Sir Guy Carleton invested him with the command of the Canadian army. Handing over the leadership of the great offensive was a bitter experience for Carleton, but he bore it with dignity. Despite his disappointment, he did everything within his power to assist Burgoyne in organizing the expedition.

The army from Canada made a brave display. About 4,000 British, 3,200 German auxiliaries from Brunswick and Hesse-Hanau, and 250 Canadian and loyalist soldiers, attended by perhaps 1,000 non-combatants and camp followers and about 400 Iroquois and Algonquian warriors from various tribes, started the fateful march southward. Their train of artillery consisted of 80 cannons, 12 howitzers, and 46 mortars—138 pieces in all. Hundreds of draft animals and carts transported thousands of barrels of provisions, supplies, army and personal baggage, and much of the artillery. For water carriage, there were dozens of canoes and hundreds of batteaux. Nine Royal Navy vessels and about 30 gunboats commanded by Commodore Skeffington Lutwidge made up the fleet on the waters of Lake Champlain that accompanied the army.

Batteaux

(PRONOUNCED "BAA-TOW," A FRENCH WORD MEANING "BOATS") WERE COMMONLY USED WATER TRANSPORTS IN THE 18TH CENTURY. THEY WERE FLAT BOTTOMED AND TRANSPORTED CARGO, TROOPS, OR COULD BE TIED AND CHAINED TOGETHER TO MAKE A PONTOON TO SUPPORT A BRIDGE STRETCHED ACROSS A RIVER. THERE WERE NO OFFICIAL DIMENSIONS FOR THESE COMMON BOATS, BUT A TYPICAL ONE WAS ABOUT 30-FEET LONG, SEVEN-FEET WIDE AND THREE-FEET DEEP.

ILLUSTRATION BY ERIC SCHNITZER,
SARATOGA NATIONAL HISTORICAL PARK

Despite problems in collecting adequate carts and a sufficient number of draft animals, the expedition got off to a good start. The preliminary objective, Crown Point, was taken on June 25. For the next week, the main part of the army and its support flotilla and train assembled for the actual opening of the campaign. On June 30, Burgoyne issued a general order that read:

> *The army embarks to-morrow, to approach the enemy.*
> *We are to contend for the King, and the constitution*
> *of Great Britain, to vindicate Law, and to relieve the*

oppressed—a cause in which his Majesty's Troops and those
of the Princes his Allies, will feel equal excitement. The serv-
ices required of this particular expedition, are critical and
conspicuous. During our progress occasions may occur, in
which no difficulty, nor labour, nor life are to be regarded.
This Army must not Retreat.

Having provided for the security of Crown Point, the troops and their popular, confident commander were now prepared to move against their first major obstacle—Fort Ticonderoga.

Ten miles south of Crown Point, Ticonderoga stands on a promontory that dominates the entrance to the southern part of Lake Champlain and the northern end of Lake George, both of which provide water routes to within a few miles of the Hudson. Built by France during The French and Indian War, the square, bastioned, stone fort had been captured in 1759 by the British, who occupied it for the next 16 years. In 1775, American forces under Colonels Ethan Allen and Benedict Arnold took it from the British and, during the months that followed, repaired and enlarged its defenses. The Americans also built new works on Mount Independence across the lake. By late June 1777 the American garrison, under Scottish-born Major General Arthur St. Clair, consisted of about 2,800 Continentals and militiamen, one-fourth the minimum number required to man the more than 2,000 yards of outer defense lines and the fort itself. Not only were there not enough men: a shortage of every necessity—food, clothing, and arms—sapped morale and undermined efficiency.

As the British approached, the American defenders watched with more apprehension than confidence. Major General Philip Schuyler, commander of the Northern Department of the Continental Army, was charged with halting the British offensive and had no illusions about the combat readiness of his troops. In a frame of mind that reflected that pessimism, he left his headquarters in Albany and presided over a council of war in the fort on June 20. Knowing that the garrison was too weak to hold the entire works, the council decided to defend the fort as long as possible and then withdraw to Mount Independence by way of the bridge that stretched across the lake. If that position became untenable, the troops would retreat southward in small boats, or batteaux. A log and chain boom, which had been laid across the channel north of the bridge to close the passage between the upper and lower ends of Lake Champlain, would prevent the British from pursuing them. Satisfied that he had provided for the defense of the "Gibraltar of the North," as Ticonderoga was called, Schuyler returned to Albany, leaving St. Clair to carry out the council's plan.

The British operations against Ticonderoga began on July 2 when a

General Burgoyne addresses the Indians.

ONE OF THE MOST CONTROVERSIAL
ACTIONS TAKEN BY GENERAL
BURGOYNE DURING HIS MILITARY
CAMPAIGN WAS THE EMPLOYMENT
OF INDIANS. OSTENSIBLY
EMPLOYED AS SCOUTS, THEIR
PRESENCE WAS NONETHELESS
A CALCULATED ATTEMPT TO
TERRORIZE THE REBELLING
AMERICANS. THE AMERICANS
FOR THEIR PART ALSO EMPLOYED
DETACHMENTS OF INDIANS,
WITH SIMILAR INTENT.

detachment of Brigadier General Simon Fraser's elite Advanced Corps, supported by loyalists and Indians, approached the American sawmills at Mount Hope. The rebel garrison set fire to the works and withdrew to the "old French lines," entrenchments that stretched across much of the promontory northwest of the fortress. Fraser remained on Mount Hope, which lay between the fort and the portage at Lake George. Some of the Indians advanced rashly upon the outerworks of the fort. British rangers under the command of Captain Alexander Fraser (nephew of the British general) and some loyalists moved to support them. They succeeded in driving off a picket of 50 Americans, but upon coming up to the old French lines, were hit hard by its defenses. The attackers withdrew with the loss of less than 10 men killed, wounded, and captured. The Americans suffered nearly 20 casualties.

On July 4, while an indecisive artillery duel depleted the American's ammunition and St. Clair received reinforcements in the form of 900 militiamen, Burgoyne deployed his forces. On the morning of the 5th, St. Clair learned that the enemy was mounting cannons on the summit of Mount Defiance, southwest of Ticonderoga. The Americans had not occupied the eminence because they thought it too steep to be scaled by artillery. Burgoyne's chief of artillery and second-in-command, Major General William Phillips, believed otherwise. "Where a goat can go, a man can go," he declared; "and where a man can go, he can drag a gun." While these cannons may not have been able to accurately hit the forts themselves, the extensive American lines of defense surrounding Fort Ticonderoga and Mount Independence could be bombarded. That night, after a heavy artillery bombardment of the British

General William Phillips

and German lines, the Americans evacuated Fort Ticonderoga. Colonel Pierce Long of New Hampshire, with about 400 men, took the supplies, invalids, and the women and children south to Skenesborough (now Whitehall, NY) by boat. St. Clair marched the rest of his army along the eastern side of the lake behind Mount Independence southeast toward Hubbardton (in present-day Vermont). From there he would move on to Castle Town (now Castleton, VT) and then west to Skenesborough to join Long.

While General Fraser's Advanced Corps, supported by some German troops under Major General Friedrich Adolph, Baron von Riedesel, pursued the main body of Americans by land, Burgoyne garrisoned Ticonderoga and set out with his British troops in pursuit of Long's flotilla. The British quickly broke through the log boom and bridge, and set out after the Americans.

While the British continued their advance south on Lake Champlain to pursue Long's flotilla, St. Clair's men, sweltering in the intense July heat, swore their way along the narrow, rough, and rutted trace that led to the small hamlet of Hubbardton. Arriving there on July 6, St. Clair drove most of his weary, disheartened soldiers another six miles to the day's objective, Castle Town. He left Colonel Seth Warner and the 150 men of Warner's own Additional Continental Regiment (The Green Mountain Boys), the 2nd New Hampshire Regiment under Colonel Nathan Hale (not the youthful patriot spy hanged by the British in 1776), and some militia at Hubbardton with orders to bring in the rear guard, consisting of the 11th Massachusetts Regiment under Colonel Ebenezer Francis and stragglers from the army.

Warner, long on courage and short on discipline, disobeyed his orders. Instead of bringing in the rear guard and marching to Castle Town, he, Francis, and Hale decided to spend the night where they were, not aware that Fraser's Advanced Corps was camped just three miles to the northwest. The next morning, July 7, while the Americans were preparing breakfast, Fraser attacked.

A British "hat" soldier from the 24th Regiment of Foot.

MOST OF BURGOYNE'S BRITISH REGIMENTS HAD ARRIVED IN CANADA IN 1776 TO DEFEND THAT COLONY AGAINST THE INVADING AMERICAN ARMY. IN 1777, BURGOYNE'S BRITISH SOLDIERS CUT THEIR FAMILIAR TRICORN HATS DOWN INTO SMALLER CAPS, AND THEIR KNEE-LENGTH WOOLEN COATS INTO SHORTER JACKETS, SO THEY WOULD BE "MORE COMMODIOUS FOR FOREST WARFARE."

COURTESY OF ERIC SCHNITZER

The Americans had posted a few sentries, but the surprise was complete. Hale and his men fled in disorder, but many were re-formed by Major Benjamin Titcomb. Warner and Francis rallied their troops, and a fierce fight began.

The heavily wooded Hubbardton area presented both sides with a frustrating maze of woods and very hilly, even mountainous terrain. Orderly unit action was difficult, but both sides made maneuvers to prevent themselves from being outflanked by their enemy. After his initial attack was abruptly halted by strong opposition, Fraser tried to turn the American left by sending most of his grenadier battalion under Major John Dyke Acland, supported by some of his light infantry battalion under Major Alexander Lindsay, 6th Earl of Balcarres, up steep Zion Hill. Warner, noticing this move, pulled his regiment back, "refusing the flank," while Francis' and Titcomb's men hit the weakened British left and center. The battle was becoming desperate for the British, as their thin left and center were being hit hard by the Americans, when a strange sound from the rear of the British line was heard. Music was playing and lusty voices were singing a German hymn: the Brunswickers had arrived.

General von Riedesel, commander of Burgoyne's German troops, and leading the Brunswickers supporting Fraser, had heard the sounds of battle as he approached Hubbardton. The 39-year-old veteran cavalryman hurried his men forward, sending his advance guard against the American right. His German jägers (pronounced "yea-gers," a German word meaning "hunters"), advancing to the inspirational sound of music, came against a vicious fire. Titcomb's and Francis' men poured volley after volley into them, but the Germans continued the attack. The Americans held their ground until a turning movement by German grenadiers and chasseurs (light infantry) enveloped their right, and Francis

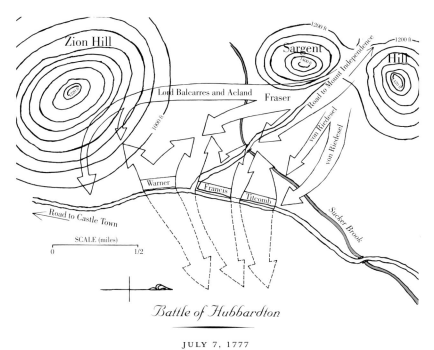

Battle of Hubbardton

JULY 7, 1777

MAP BY ERIC SCHNITZER, SARATOGA NATIONAL HISTORICAL PARK

was killed. Fraser's soldiers delivered a successful bayonet charge, and the Americans broke and disappeared into the woods. Warner's men, their right exposed, could stand no longer. At Warner's command, they evaporated into the wilderness to meet and reform at Manchester, south of Hubbardton.

At Castle Town, St. Clair heard the sounds of battle, but he had no hymn-singing professionals to send back to support his men at Hubbardton. What he did have were two militia regiments, which, with their customary cavalier attitude toward discipline, had dropped out of the line of march and encamped two miles from Hubbardton. St. Clair's aides ordered them to go to Warner's assistance, but they refused and hastily rejoined the main column toward which they had acted so independently the day before. While trying to organize a relief force among his soldiers, whose reluctance increased with the arrival of the insubordinate militia, St. Clair learned of Warner's defeat. The issue was settled—the Americans would continue their withdrawal.

Meanwhile, Colonel Long's flotilla, retreating from Ticonderoga, reached Skenesborough on July 6, closely pursued by the main part of Burgoyne's army. One look at the place convinced Long that it could not be defended

General Friedrich Adolph, Baron von Riedesel

(1738–1800) PICTURED HERE
AT THE TIME OF HIS
MARRIAGE IN 1762.
COMMANDER OF THE GERMAN
CONTINGENT OF BURGOYNE'S
ARMY, HE WAS OFTEN
RELEGATED TO SUPPORTING
ASSIGNMENTS. HOWEVER,
DESPITE BARRIERS OF
LANGUAGE AND BRITISH
PREJUDICE AGAINST THE
GERMANS, RIEDESEL
DEMONSTRATED SOLID
ABILITIES AS A COMMANDER.

against a strong enemy attack. After setting fire to whatever would burn, including most of the supplies, and abandoning everything else, he and his small force set out quickly for Fort Anne (now Fort Ann, NY), about 11 miles to the south on Wood Creek.

Burgoyne entered Skenesborough that same day, and sent Lieutenant Colonel John Hill with a part of the 9th Regiment of Foot in pursuit of Long, who reached Fort Anne before the British could intercept him. Fortunately for the Americans, Hill's advance was slowed by the nearly impassable road, and it was the evening of the 7th before the British reached a position one mile from the fort. Early the next morning, an American entered Hill's camp, claimed to be a deserter, and told Hill that Long had 1,000 men in the fort. Because he had only 190 men, Hill sent back for reinforcements. The "deserter" noted Hill's weakness and promptly slipped away to report it to Long. By this time, Colonel Henry Van Rensselaer with 400 New York militia had reinforced Long, and the Americans attacked the British where they were encamped on a narrow, wooded shelf of land between the creek and a steep, 500-foot-high ridge. To avoid being surrounded, Hill's men scrambled up the ridge and held the Americans at bay for nearly two hours. Just when the British were running out of ammunition and were under attack from all sides, they heard an Indian war whoop. The Americans heard it too. Short on ammunition and having no desire to take on a fresh war party, they beat a hasty retreat, setting fire to the fort as they withdrew.

There had been a war cry, but there were no Indians—just one lone British officer, Captain John Money. He had been sent with a party of Indians to support Hill, and when the Indians lagged behind, the captain went on ahead. When he reached the scene of the fighting and saw Hill's predicament, he

*An Algonquian
warrior serving with
Burgoyne's army.*

THE ALGONQUIANS THAT
SERVED CAME FROM MANY
VARIOUS TRIBES, SOME
CLAIMING TO HAVE
TRAVELED OVER 1,000
MILES TO JOIN BURGOYNE.
DURING THE REVOLUTION,
MANY OF THE ALGONQUIAN
TRIBES LOOSELY ALLIED
THEMSELVES WITH SOME OF
THEIR ANCIENT ENEMIES—
THE IROQUOIS.

COURTESY OF ERIC SCHNITZER

gambled and gave the yell. The ruse worked.

In the light of Long's withdrawal and the defeat at Hubbardton, all that St. Clair could do was to try to save his army by making a long detour around Skenesborough and retreat to Fort Edward. This "fort," a small village with a dilapidated colonial war fortification, was about 12 miles south of Fort Anne at the portage between Wood Creek and the Hudson River. He arrived there on July 12 and was met by Schuyler, who took personal command of the field operations. By this time, Schuyler was under fire for the loss of Ticonderoga, but his army was neither physically nor psychologically capable of stopping the British. Under the circumstances, he had no option but to continue the retreat.

While at Skenesborough, Burgoyne decided upon his next move. He had a choice of two routes southward—one by way of going back to Ticonderoga and then using Lake George, another by way of using the small waterway called Wood Creek from Skenesborough to the Hudson River, a distance of about 23 miles. He chose the latter, basing his decision on five factors. First, Lake George is 221 feet above Lake Champlain, and he would have to drag his artillery, supplies, and boats up this rise through a connecting gorge five miles long. Second, if he chose the Lake George route, he would alert the Americans to the fact that he was not threatening New England. By keeping east of the lake, he believed he was confusing them concerning his objective. Third, the Americans were retreating toward Castle Town, and if he expected to catch them, he would have to move south and east, unless he could be certain that by advancing via Lake George he would cut them off before they reached the Hudson. Fourth, the Lake George route had two portages, whereas the other route had only one. Finally, heading back on Lake Champlain north to Ticonderoga could look like a retreat to the Americans. Burgoyne felt he had the initiative, and didn't want to lose it.

Philip Schuyler was not about to allow Burgoyne an easy march south toward the Hudson River. He ordered his second-in-command of the engi-

Colonel Tadeusz Kosciuszko

(1746–1817) A 31-YEAR-OLD
ENGINEER FROM POLAND
WHO VOLUNTEERED HIS
SERVICES FOR THE AMERICAN
CAUSE. KOSCIUSZKO'S
FORTIFICATIONS ERECTED ON
BEMIS HEIGHTS WERE
A FACTOR IN CHANNELING
THE BRITISH ARMY'S
MANEUVERING.

COURTESY EMBASSY OF
THE REPUBLIC OF POLAND

neers, Colonel Andrzej Tadeusz Bonawentura Kosciuszko (known as Thaddeus Kosciuszko, pronounced "Kos-shoos-ko"), to delay the British advance. Under Kosciuszko's direction, hundreds of American workmen destroyed bridges, felled trees, put obstructions into Wood Creek, and flooded roads (little more than dirt wagon paths) and other areas by diverting streams. Burgoyne's army would struggle through the next 23 miles. This leg of the journey would take almost as many days, with the army battling the July sun to overcome these numerous obstacles and delays.

Burgoyne's army began reaching Fort Edward in the last days of July. While the Americans were exchanging territory for time, the British supply problem was growing more acute as their line of communication lengthened. Upon arriving at Fort Edward on the Hudson River, Burgoyne decided to remedy his situation by sending a force into the Connecticut River country, which, according to a report from his German commander, Baron von Riedesel, was rich in food and livestock. The British commander planned the expedition to start at the mouth of the Batten Kill (a Dutch word meaning "creek"), move eastward across the Green Mountains to the Connecticut Valley, remain there long enough to encourage local loyalists, enlist men for a loyalist corps, collect horses and supplies, and rejoin the army at Albany in about two weeks. As Burgoyne defined the mission, "The objective... is to try the affections of the country, to disconcert the councils of the enemy, to mount the [von] Riedesel's dragoons, to compleat Peter's Corps [of loyalists], and to obtain large supplies of cattle, horses, and carriages." This force was also expected to secure all of the saddles, bridles, wagons, and draft oxen it could find, as well as arrest anyone "acting" as rebel officers or in rebel governments.

Considering the nature of the country and the purpose of the expedition, the composition of the force committed was remarkable. The commander was Lieutenant Colonel Friedrich Baum, whose 230 unmounted Brunswick dra-

A private soldier of Jessup's Rangers,

goons of the Regiment Prinz Ludwig were the centerpiece of a force that included 150 more German troops, 60 British rangers, and 170 loyalists, Canadians, and Indians. They also had two small 3-pound cannons. Because the only language Baum could speak was German, Baron von Riedesel assigned German-speaking British officers, as well as his own personal aide-de-camp Captain Laurentius O'Connell of the Brunswick Guards, to act as interpreters. If Baum, a German officer who did not know the country or its inhabitants, was ill suited to lead such an expedition, the decision to use dismounted dragoons was the height of folly. The mission demanded speed in a wooded, hilly region where the roads were nearly impassable to troops in any but the driest of weather. The dragoons were not meant to act as infantry, and their cumbersome swords and large hats only made it more difficult for them to move rapidly on foot.

Baum's force set out on August 9. Shortly afterward, Burgoyne learned that the Americans had a large supply depot at Bennington in the Hampshire Grants (present-day Vermont). This seemed like a godsend for his shortage-plagued army, and Bennington was much nearer at hand than the riches of the Connecticut Valley. Burgoyne rode after Baum the next day and directed him to change his objective.

Defending Bennington were about 1,500 New Hampshire militiamen under Brigadier General John Stark. A proud and experienced soldier, Stark had served in the famous Roger's Rangers during The French and Indian War. In 1775, he had distinguished himself in the Battle of Bunker Hill outside Boston. The next year he gained additional laurels in the Canadian campaign and at Trenton and Princeton. Angered at being passed over for promotion early in 1777, he had resigned from the army and retired to his New Hampshire farm.

When Burgoyne launched his invasion of the northern frontier, the New Hampshire Legislature called upon Stark to organize a brigade to help meet the British threat. He agreed, but only on the condition that the brigade consist solely of New Hampshire men and that he be allowed to use it as he saw fit, independent of the Continental Congress and of the Continental Army. In short, he would be accountable only to the New Hampshire Legislature. The legislature accepted Stark's terms and commissioned him a brigadier general.

During the first week of August 1777, Stark's brigade lay at Manchester in the Hampshire Grants, where the remnants of Seth Warner's Continentals had gathered to reorganize after their defeat at Hubbardton. After refusing to join General Schuyler's army on the Hudson, Stark marched his men south to Bennington and reached there on the 8th. There he learned of Baum's advance, and on the 13th he sent about 210 men west to delay it.

On August 14, a day after leaving the Hudson, Baum's column encountered Stark's detachment near Van Schaick's gristmill on the Walloomsac River in St. Croix (or San Coick, now North Hoosick, NY). After harassing Baum's men, the Americans withdrew toward Bennington and joined their main body. Baum set out in pursuit. From information he received from American captives, Baum learned that he was outnumbered by more than two to one, but the German colonel believed the Americans would flee upon his arrival. Local people, professing to be loyalists, flocked to Baum's little army and requested that he arm them.

The two forces met about four miles west of Bennington later that same day, where a small bridge crossed the Walloomsac River. Stark, who had already sent word to Manchester for Warner's men to advance to Bennington, posted his troops on one side of the river, while Baum positioned his on the other. There was heavy skirmishing throughout the day, and Baum's small cannons proved useful as they drove the Americans away. Baum then quickly wrote to Burgoyne, requesting reinforcements. He still seemed confident, even though it was apparent that the Americans would not flee, and did not indicate in his letter that he was in any real danger.

The German commander knew that the bridge was a critical point, and on the next day he sent 200 loyalists across the river to throw up a breastwork. There, on a rise of ground south of the bridge, they erected a fortification later called the Tory Redoubt. Canadians took up positions in small buildings on both sides of the bridge. Two smaller works were built to cover the bridge, where a 3-pound cannon and about 50 German grenadiers and British rangers were posted. Many of the dragoons, along with the other 3-pounder, occupied a large fieldwork later called the Dragoon Redoubt on the eminence overlooking the river. Sixty jägers and chasseurs occupied a position on the riverbank. The rest of the loyalists, German grenadiers, and the Indians assembled near the baggage of the detachment in a field southwest of the Dragoon Redoubt, forming a rear guard.

A grenadier of the Brunswick Regiment Specht

After some skirmishing in the morning, Stark's and Baum's men lay in their positions, soaked by the heavy rain that continued throughout the day. The rain stopped on the morning of the 16th, and Stark began a double envelopment, or complete encirclement, of Baum's position. The northern element of this pincer movement, more than 300 men under the command of Colonel Moses Nichols of New Hampshire, marched through the woods and attacked the Dragoon Redoubt at about 3 p.m. As Nichols' men began the attack, the western element of 300 more men under a Vermonter, Colonel Samuel Herrick, which had marched about five miles undetected to the back of the enemy's positions, struck Baum's rear guard and rushed up to the Dragoon Redoubt, joining Nichols' men. A third column of 200 men under Colonels David Hobart and Thomas Stickney of New Hampshire moved out of Stark's camp and executed a double envelopment in miniature of the Tory Redoubt. At the same time, Stark marched a force of more than 300 men down the road directly toward the bridge in the enemy's center.

From his post near the bridge, Colonel Baum watched as contingents of Americans moved toward his positions, and now heard growing sounds of ever increasing musket fire. The day before he had allowed the local inhabitants to tour through his camp and leave as they wished. Baum had neglected to order the posting of sentinels and guards, and he had not even visited or inspected the post of the Dragoon Redoubt on the eminence that it topped. The Indians, realizing the danger of the situation, moved to the supposed safety of the Dragoon Redoubt.

The men in the Tory Redoubt were attacked and routed after a brief resistance. The force in the Dragoon Redoubt held its ground against the attack until they were overwhelmed by superior numbers, and fled down the hill. The Indians had gone before them, down the hill and through the woods, and did not participate in the ensuing melee. The troops

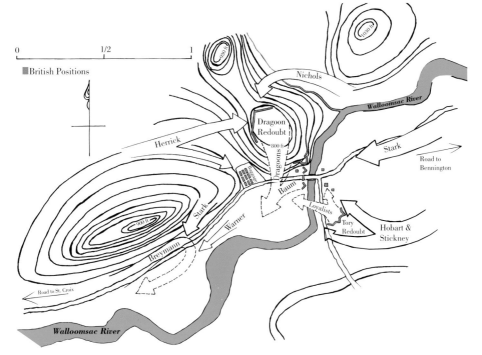

First and Second Battles of Bennington

AUGUST 16, 1777

MAP BY ERIC SCHNITZER, SARATOGA NATIONAL HISTORICAL PARK

covering the bridge and riverbank were now attacked from the front and both flanks, but held as best they could. When their ammunition ran out the dragoons, rallying around their commander, drew their swords and started to cut their way through the Americans. Most of Stark's men lacked bayonets and the Germans were making good progress as they attempted to flee to the rear when Baum was mortally wounded. The greatly outnumbered dragoons gave up the fight at about 4 o'clock.

Lieutenant Colonel Heinrich Breymann's corps, sent out by Burgoyne in response to Baum's earlier call on the 14th for reinforcements, left their camp at 9 a.m. on the 15th for the 24-mile march to aid Baum. Breymann's corps, 660 men strong with two 6-pound cannons, reached Van Schaick's Gristmill—about two miles west of where the battle had just wound down—at about 4:30 p.m. There, Breymann met refugees from Baum's command who gave confusing and contradictory accounts of the battle. But the tired Germans continued their march, fighting off militia attempts to stop them.

Stark was in poor condition to meet Breymann. Many of his men had scat-

tered to loot and to chase fugitives. But Seth Warner's Continentals had arrived from Bennington and helped the rallied militia pitch into Breymann's troops about one mile west of the river crossing. Although both forces had made an exhausting march in wet and muggy weather, they fought vigorously. When the Germans had exhausted nearly all of their ammunition, Breymann ordered a withdrawal. The Americans, however, pushed his troops furiously from all sides. Breymann, who was wounded in the leg, succeeded in leading a retreat through the night that saved more than three-quarters of his relief force. Stark and Warner ordered their men to break contact on account of the darkness and withdrew back towards Bennington.

The Americans reaped a rich harvest in booty, including four cannons, several wagons, and hundreds of muskets, rifles, and swords. Baum and Breymann lost about 900 men—most of whom were captured. Burgoyne would have to do without the supplies at Bennington. The American casualties are unknown, because Stark never submitted a report, but they probably amounted to about 50. The victory was a great boost to patriot morale at a time when such a boost was desperately needed. The fortunes of war had begun to turn.

Almost simultaneous with the British failure at Bennington was another on the Mohawk River that helped to doom Burgoyne's campaign. Part of the invasion plan provided for an expedition to move down the Mohawk River and meet Burgoyne at Albany. That expedition, which left Oswego on Lake Ontario on July 26, consisted of about 280 British and German regulars, 470 loyalists and Canadians, and 800 Iroquois and Algonquian warriors. The commander was Lieutenant Colonel Barry St. Leger, member of an old Anglo-Irish family with a long, honorable record of service to the Crown. He requested and received the "local" rank of Brigadier General.

The principal American defense work on the Mohawk River was Fort Stanwix (called Fort Schuyler by the Americans). It was a strong earthen and moated installation constructed of logs at the river's headwaters, which guarded The Great Oneida Carrying Place that linked the river with the water route to Lake Ontario. The fort was garrisoned by the 400-man 3rd New York Continental Regiment, 150 men from Colonel James Wesson's 9th Massachusetts Regiment, a small detachment of the 2nd Continental Artillery, and 100 New York militiamen. Twenty-eight-year-old Colonel Peter Gansevoort was in overall command.

St. Leger's troops arrived at the fort on August 2 and soon after began siege operations. Meanwhile, militia Brigadier General Nicholas Herkimer had learned of St. Leger's advance and collected men from the Tryon County militias to go to Gansevoort's relief. En route, the militia were ambushed on August 6 near Oriskany, about six miles southeast of the fort and, after a desperate hand-to-hand fight in which Herkimer was mortally wounded, with-

General Benedict Arnold

drew with heavy losses. During the battle, Lieutenant Colonel Marinus Willett, second-in-command at Fort Stanwix, led a sortie against St. Leger's virtually undefended camp. This action may not have alleviated Herkimer's predicament, but Willett's men captured a large quantity of the enemy's supplies. The British maintained the siege, but they were badly weakened.

Despite the ease with which St. Leger was able to besiege Fort Stanwix, General Schuyler had not neglected the defense of the Mohawk Valley. During July he had tried to obtain additional Continental troops for the western frontier of his command and sought New York State's assistance in finding militia units that could be sent up the river to oppose just such a movement as that undertaken by St. Leger. He had also written letters of advice and encouragement to General Herkimer and the Tryon County Committee of Safety.

Schuyler's involvement in the defense of Fort Stanwix took a more concrete form when, on August 12, he sent units of Brigadier General Ebenezer Learned's brigade to raise the siege. On August 13, Arthur St. Clair left for Philadelphia to answer congressional charges of near-treason for the evacuation of Ticonderoga. That same day, Major General Benedict Arnold left the main body of Schuyler's army at Stillwater, where it had been since early August, to take command of American forces in the Mohawk Valley.

Advancing rapidly to German Flats, about 30 miles east of the Oriskany battlefield, Arnold's men captured a number of loyalists, one of whom was a

General Philip Schuyler

mentally deficient man named Hon Yost Schuyler, a distant relative of General Schuyler. Sentenced to death as a spy, Hon Yost was reprieved on the condition that he spread the rumor among St. Leger's Indians that the Americans were advancing in overwhelming numbers. The ploy worked. The Indians, who constituted about one-half of St. Leger's force and who had joined the expedition with the expectation of little fighting and much loot, completely deserted. St. Leger abandoned operations and retreated to Canada.

Except for the battles near Bennington, there had been little about the defense of the Champlain-George-Hudson line to inspire confidence and pride among those who were fighting for independence. There had been few heroic stands. In fact, since the loss of Skenesborough on July 6, the Americans had usually maintained a distance of several miles between the two armies. But the Northern Department's army had slowed the pace of the British advance by felling trees, destroying bridges, and denying the enemy the use of crops and livestock along the route southward. More important, by exchanging territory for time, the Americans had shortened their own communication lines while lengthening those of the enemy. They also had more men and supplies available to them, while Burgoyne had to forage off a countryside that was often unfriendly.

Beginning on August 10, Schuyler began a slow withdrawal from Stillwater to Van Schaick's and Haver Islands (now Peebles Island), where the Mohawk River empties into the Hudson. For weeks, Schuyler was the object of a rising chorus of criticism and abuse. His lack of aggressiveness, the way he directed much of the defensive operations from the comfort of his Albany and Saratoga homes, the loss of Ticonderoga, the hostility of New Englanders who dis-

General Horatio Gates

(1728–1806) A FORMER
BRITISH MAJOR, GATES BROUGHT
VALUABLE PROFESSIONAL
EXPERIENCE TO THE FLEDGLING
CONTINENTAL ARMY. GATES'
MAIN ABILITIES WERE FOUND IN
ADMINISTRATION, BUT HIS
COMMAND OF THE NORTHERN
ARMY OWED MUCH TO FACTIONAL
DISPUTES IN CONGRESS.

COURTESY INDEPENDENCE NATIONAL
HISTORICAL PARK

trusted his Dutch heritage, military ability, and political views, and his frigidly aristocratic manner united to bring him the censure of civil and military leaders. The Americans were afraid that the British were going to win in the North, and they clamored for a more aggressive commander.

As it had in 1776 and earlier in 1777, the command of the Northern Department of the Continental Army again became the subject of debate in Congress. It was an old issue that had long troubled civilian leaders and aggravated personal, political, and sectional tensions. Once again, it involved the same two men who, between them, had borne the hopes and frustrations of command on the northern frontier— Philip John Schuyler, Hudson Valley patrician and political leader, and Horatio Gates, former British army officer turned Virginia planter.

Schuyler had been appointed to command the Northern Department on June 19, 1775. A week later he was charged with leading an offensive up the Champlain-Hudson route against Canada. Plagued by gout, Schuyler turned over the field command to Brigadier General Richard Montgomery, who was killed in an unsuccessful, climactic attack on Québec City. When the invasion failed and the Americans were forced to retreat from Canada in the spring of 1776, many soldiers and politicians blamed Schuyler for the defeat. Because of the rising criticism of the New York commander, Congress on June 17 appointed Major General Horatio Gates, then adjutant general of the Continental Army, commander of the American forces in Canada.

Gates arrived at Schuyler's headquarters in Albany believing that he was to exercise complete command over the Northern Department. Schuyler refused to recognize Gates' jurisdiction, however, pointing out that the congressional resolutions and Washington's instructions limited Gates' authority to operations in Canada. Since the army was then in New York, Schuyler maintained that he was still in command of the department. Pending clarification of their respective positions, Gates acquiesced and submitted to Schuyler's authority.

After Congress confirmed Schuyler's interpretation in July, Gates remained in the north as commander at Ticonderoga. As the next ranking senior officer under Schuyler, he also functioned as second-in-command of the Northern Department. Both Schuyler and Gates tried to adjust to this less-than-ideal situation, but their personalities and perspectives sometimes made this difficult. Schuyler was an aloof, class-conscious conservative. Although Gates had grown up on the fringes of English upper-class society and had been a career officer in the British army before the war, he was more democratic, both socially and politically. Sectionalism compounded their difficulties. New Englanders, whose attitudes toward Schuyler ran from critical to hostile, found Gates much more congenial and effective. Schuyler's much-publicized lack of aggressiveness and the military misfortunes attending northern operations earned him many critics in the army and Congress who considered Gates a more professional officer and the kind of commander the important northern frontier required.

Late in 1776, at the direction of Congress, Gates led the Pennsylvania and New Jersey troops at Ticonderoga south to join Washington for the campaign in New Jersey. For some time Gates commanded at Philadelphia, and was requested by Washington and Congress to return to his old job as adjutant general of the army, which he declined. In the meantime, Congress had again grown dissatisfied with Schuyler and was determined to replace him. On March 25, 1777, John Hancock, president of the Continental Congress, ordered Gates to assume an independent command of the American forces at Fort Ticonderoga, which comprised most of the forces in the Northern Department. Almost two months later, however, after having been convinced of the importance of keeping the Northern Department under one commander, Congress reversed itself and returned the command of the fort to Schuyler. Thus Schuyler commanded the northern frontier when Burgoyne began his offensive.

The loss of Ticonderoga and the apparent success of the British advance provided Schuyler's critics with ammunition to further question his military capabilities and to gain converts from among those who had supported the general in the past, including some who were looking for a scapegoat on whom to place the blame for American failures. After a debate that sometimes revealed as much about sectional and political loyalties as it did an awareness of military problems, Congress asked General Washington to select a new northern commander. The commander-in-chief politely declined. Congressional delegates then, by secret ballot, chose Gates by a vote of 11 states. Schuyler afterward demanded a court martial to clear his reputation. Acquitted of charges of incompetence, he resigned his commission on April 19, 1779.

Gates has been charged with intrigue in securing the command, but he was no more active in advancing his interests than his rival. Just why he should have conspired to obtain command in a department where he had already suffered extensive frustrations is not clear. It certainly did not hold much promise of glory; and the prospects in mid-summer of 1777 seemed to portend failure, not success. There were less controversial and more secure posts, and if Gates enjoyed the political influence attributed to him by his critics, he could have had any one of them.

Gates took command of the Northern Department on August 19, 1777, and immediately attacked the army's problems with professional vigor. He sent letters to the executives and legislatures of New York and New England asking for militia and supplies. He improved the medical services, long a scandal. He tried to persuade John Stark, who heretofore refused to be bound by any authority other than the New Hampshire Legislature, to integrate his militia into the department. When that failed, Gates bluntly reminded Stark that failure to act for the general good would tarnish the glory he had won at Bennington. The result was that Stark gave limited and sporadic cooperation.

By early September, Gates matured a strategy for defeating Burgoyne. The terrain at the Mohawk-Hudson River junction was too flat and open to provide good defensive positions. He therefore decided to move the main part of his army back north to Stillwater where he would have a better chance of blocking Burgoyne's march to Albany. Militia and Continental units under Major General Benjamin Lincoln, second-in-command under Gates, and Stark were directed to operate east and north of Fort Edward along Burgoyne's lengthy and vulnerable line of communication.

At Stillwater, Gates found that the distance between the river and the hills was too great to meet his requirements for a defensive position, so he moved his troops three miles northward to the heights behind Jotham Bemis' tavern, where a bend in the river forced the road to Albany against the base of the hills. The Americans arrived at Bemis Heights on September 12 and began to build entrenchments that blocked the road and fortified the bluffs. Under the supervision of Colonel Thaddeus Kosciuszko, Gates' men laid out fortifications along the crest of the bluffs above the road. They built the main line of entrenchments from a ravine behind the bluffs west to John Neilson's farm on the crest of the heights, and extended it southwest for about three-quarters of a mile. They posted their 22 cannons at strategic points, and pickets manned several outposts north and west of the fortified camp. The Americans were digging in; the next move was up to Burgoyne.

The Battles of Saratoga

By the time Burgoyne invaded the northern frontier, the land along the Hudson River below Fort Edward had been settled and under cultivation for more than half a century. The alluvial flats were dotted with farms and woodlots that varied in size according to the number of people available to carry out the arduous work of clearing and cultivating farms in a wooded region. Most of the farmers held indentures from owners of old and extensive patents. In many cases, these were of such long duration that they almost amounted to ownership by the occupant.

Most of the houses were modest in size and design, often one-story or one-and-a-half story buildings that resembled the older homes of western New England or the Dutch areas to the south. There were several sawmills on the streams that empty into the river. Most of the houses on the flats were frame, similar to John Neilson's home on Bemis Heights. An occasional house, like the Woodworth home, where Gates had his headquarters while the American army encamped at Bemis Heights, was more prestigious, with a gambrel roof and extensive outbuildings. The most impressive home north of the old Schuyler family seat at "The Flatts" in Albany was General Schuyler's country house at Saratoga (now Schuylerville, NY). Barns and outbuildings were usually log and less impressive than contemporary German types in Pennsylvania. The Dutch who moved upstream and the Quakers and Congregationalists who came either up the river or from New England were, generally, a thrifty, industrious lot, and they had been in the region long enough to make the valley floor agrarian rather than wilderness in character.

The hills above the valley had been settled later, due to the poorer soil. There, houses were cruder and often made of logs. Outbuildings and barns were more primitive; fields less extensive; and the woods denser. This was new country that retained more of the wilderness character, and it bordered an even wilder backcountry.

Villages and hamlets had grown up around the old forts and blockhouses at places like Fort Edward, Saratoga, and Stillwater. They resembled their counterparts in other sections of the northern colonies. Most of them had a church or meetinghouse. Many had a school. They were agricultural centers; mills, shops, and taverns were their business establishments. Typically, most of the inhabitants, including the miller, shopkeeper, and tavernkeeper, were also farmers and supporters of the Revolution.

Several loyalist families lived around Fort Edward and there were others scattered about the area; but most of the people living along the upper Hudson sided with the rebels, not the British.

Despite the farms and settlements, the dominant feature of the country

American river fortifications, below Bemis Heights.

THESE FORTIFICATIONS WERE ERECTED SOON AFTER THE AMERICAN ARMY
MOVED UP FROM STILLWATER TO BEMIS HEIGHTS ON SEPTEMBER 12,
1777. THESE DEFENSES WERE SOME OF THE MOST IMPORTANT TO THE
AMERICANS, SINCE IT COVERED THE RIVER ROAD, ON WHICH BURGOYNE
EXPECTED TO MARCH SOUTH TO ALBANY. THE HEIGHTS THEMSELVES
ARE SHOWN, WITH FORTIFICATIONS ON THEM.

ILLUSTRATION BY RON SAPORITO, SARATOGA NATIONAL HISTORICAL PARK

was the vast forest of hardwoods and pines that stretched for hundreds of miles north, east, and west of the river. Most of these were mature woods, except for old fields that had been cultivated by the Mahicans (or Mohicans) until they were displaced by Mohawk warriors of the Iroquois Confederacy, before European settlement of the area. Large stream junctions made excellent sites for campgrounds or villages, where generations of Mahicans had lived occasionally or permanently. Game, fish, and primitive woodland farming had sustained these people until the coming of the Europeans produced the fur trade, of which they were the great entrepreneurs.

The farms and hamlets were connected by a surprising number of roads—or what passed for roads. They ran in all directions, usually at the whim of the people they served. Some went south, connecting the area with Albany

THE BATTLES OF SARATOGA

and the old Dutch villages downriver. Others ran roughly east and west, away from the river toward farms and settlements in the hills. Some of the roads running eastward provided links with the Hampshire Grants and western Massachusetts. But the Hudson River was the major highway, providing the easiest, cheapest, and most reliable north-south transportation.

After the Battles of Bennington, Burgoyne stayed on the east bank of the Hudson collecting supplies. He knew that when he resumed his advance and crossed the river he would have to abandon his communications with the north. His army waited in and around Fort Edward for well over a month. He had no opportunity of sending independent detachments to the countryside to collect food, material, and draft animals for his army. He had lost nearly one thousand Germans, loyalists, and Indians at Bennington, and there were few prospects of replacing any of those troops, save for some loyalist recruits. However, on September 4 approximately 200 Mohawk refugees joined Burgoyne after their settlement was laid to waste by American forces. They were entire families of men, women, and children of the Wolf Clan from Fort Hunter (a village where the Schoharie Creek empties into the Mohawk River, roughly 50 miles southwest of Burgoyne's army).

By September 11, Burgoyne had accumulated five weeks worth of provisions and was ready to move. On September 13, most of his army crossed the Hudson over a floating bridge, made up of boats, just above Saratoga, about 11 miles north of where the Americans were preparing defenses. Slowly Burgoyne's entire army moved southward along the river road, while the batteaux floated alongside them carrying baggage, food, and supplies. On the morning of the 19th, they were encamped at Thomas Swords' house, three miles north of Bemis Heights.

To understand the events of the next four weeks, it is necessary to keep Burgoyne's and Gates' objectives firmly in mind. Gates had a deceptively simple goal: block the British advance. The longer he could do that, the more probable would be Burgoyne's failure, for the British general had to reach his objective, Albany, before winter. His army could not survive on the northern Hudson without supplies and shelter. Gates had access to stores in Albany and New England, and could remain in his position indefinitely. But Bemis Heights was the last good defensive position; Gates was determined to end the British advance toward Albany here.

September 19 dawned unusually warm, and a fog hung over the river as Burgoyne faced a situation that every good commander tries to avoid—being forced to act on his opponent's terms. Two choices lay before him: he could keep his army in a column on the road and try to force his way through the American guns on the bluffs and the batteries on the river flats; or he could attack the Americans in their fortified camp on Bemis Heights. Retreat was a third alternative, but Burgoyne did not consider it. In any event, the militia under Lincoln, Stark, and Colonel John Brown were ready to turn the route to the north into a succession of ambushes; and Gates, whose army was now about equal in strength to Burgoyne's, could pursue the British with more ease and safety than they could retreat. The 65 miles back to Ticonderoga would have been a nightmare, even if Burgoyne succeeded in reaching the fort, which was highly unlikely.

The first alternative offered little or no hope for success. Burgoyne might have been able to drive the Americans out of the river batteries, but the fortified line on the bluffs was secure against an army in the valley. Any force marching broadside to that line probably could not have survived an attempt to move through the narrow passage between the heights and the river.

That left only the second alternative— to get the Americans out of their fortified camp and open the way to Albany. The tactic that Burgoyne employed was a movement of three columns south toward the American position, whose extent and strength were unknown to him. General Fraser's Advanced Corps, as well as most of the loyalists and Indians, made up the right column consisting of 2,400 men. Breymann's corps of 530 men formed the reserve behind them. The center column consisted of the 1,700 British troops of the army's right wing under Brigadier General James Hamilton; Burgoyne accompanied this column. The left wing of the army, numbering slightly more than 1,600 Germans under General von Riedesel, headed the left column. General Phillips, who brought up the artificers (skilled workmen), the park of artillery (uncommitted reserve artillery), hospital, army baggage, and the balance of the camp followers followed behind them with nearly 1,000 more people. The batteaux and the small detachment of

A woman camp follower.

A CERTAIN NUMBER OF WOMEN WERE ALLOWED TO FOLLOW THE ARMIES OF THE 18TH CENTURY WITH THEIR HUSBANDS AND CHILDREN. THEY WERE SEEN AS MORE A NECESSITY IN MILITARY OPERATIONS RATHER THAN AN OBSTACLE. CAMP FOLLOWERS WERE EMPLOYED OR GIVEN TASKS SUCH AS SEWING, NURSING, OR COOKING. THEY WOULD SOMETIMES HELP ON THE FIELD OF BATTLE BY DISTRIBUTING MUSKET CARTRIDGES AND STRIPPING USEFUL SUPPLIES FROM THE DEAD SOLDIERS.

ILLUSTRATION BY ERIC SCHNITZER, SARATOGA NATIONAL HISTORICAL PARK

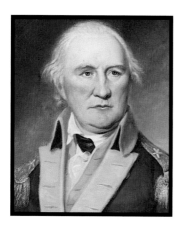

Colonel Daniel Morgan

the Royal Navy floated down the river beside the 290-man 47th Regiment. The 590-man Hesse-Hanau Regiment Erbprinz was left behind at Swords' house as a rear guard.

Fraser's and Breymann's corps marched along a road running westward from Swords' house to a point three miles from the river, and then turned southward. Hamilton's column followed Fraser's a short distance, then turned south on the first road that led down into the Great Ravine, crossed it, and moved west to a point north of John Freeman's farm. Baron von Riedesel's and Phillips' commands made up the largest of the three columns, which marched south along the river road. When the columns reached their assigned positions, a signal gun coordinated a simultaneous movement against the American camp.

Learning of the enemy's movements, Gates ordered Colonel Daniel Morgan's Rifle Regiment and Major Henry Dearborn's light infantry battalion (together called Morgan's corps, and commanded by Morgan) to reconnoiter the woods and fields north of the American lines. They were soon followed by the 1st, 2nd, and 3rd New Hampshire regiments as well as the two militia regiments from Connecticut and the 2nd and 4th New York regiments from Brigadier General Enoch Poor's brigade, which was a part of Benedict Arnold's division. At about noon, a part of Morgan's corps fired upon and killed or wounded most of the advance guard of Hamilton's center column in the Freeman farm clearing. Morgan's corps rushed forward to pursue the survivors but were outflanked by units from Fraser's Advanced Corps and dispersed, while the British survivors of the advance guard were accidentally hit by fire from their own men as they rushed back to the center column. The British drove Morgan's corps into the woods south of the farm, where they scattered, but

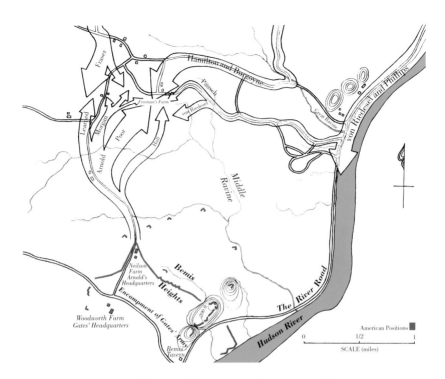

First Battle of Saratoga: Freeman's Farm

SEPTEMBER 19, 1777

MAP BY ERIC SCHNITZER, SARATOGA NATIONAL HISTORICAL PARK

were soon re-organized.

After a brief lull, during which the New Hampshire regiments joined Morgan's corps, the fight resumed. As it intensified, the other regiments of Poor's brigade, followed by Brigadier General Ebenezer Learned's brigade, also from Arnold's division, and a detachment of "volunteers" under Major William Hull of the 8th Massachusetts Regiment reinforced the Americans. The 10th Massachusetts Regiment from Brigadier General John Paterson's brigade was engaged in skirmishing with units of Fraser's Advanced Corps. Morgan's corps and Poor's brigade bore the brunt of the fight, while most of the other units faced Fraser and prevented him from going to Hamilton's full support.

For more than three hours the battle surged back and forth across the weed-grown, stump-studded farm. This was no fight between professionals and raw backwoodsmen. The greater part of the American soldiers were veteran Continental regulars, many of whom were in their third year of service. The

The Battle of Freeman's Farm.

troops deployed, attacked, retreated, rallied, and attacked again in a disciplined, soldierly manner. The British enjoyed an important advantage with their artillery, for the Americans brought none onto the field; but so persistently did Morgan's marksmen pick off the gunners that they were almost wiped out, and the guns were captured repeatedly. Because Gates' troops had nothing to discharge the cannons nor horses to move them, the guns were each time retaken and turned against the Americans.

The British regiments upheld the great traditions of their service, counterattacking again and again against increasingly heavy odds. Time and again, Burgoyne exposed himself to enemy fire. General Phillips, thinking he was needed on the field of battle, rode to Freeman's farm and led the 20th Regiment to the relief of the 62nd (which were both part of Hamilton's column) when the latter unit was being overwhelmed. But all the gallantry and skill were inadequate to counter the Americans' numerical advantage. For the British, time was running out.

At about 5 o'clock, responding to an urgent order from Burgoyne, von Riedesel started toward the Freeman farm with his own regiment, two companies of the Regiment von Rhetz, and two 6-pounders from Captain Georg Päusch's Hesse-Hanau artillery, leaving about 1,000 of his German troops on the river road. They reached the field of battle at dusk, just in time for von Riedesel to throw his fresh troops, who were again singing hymns, against the American right flank and bolster the British who were slowly retreating to the woods north of the farm. The British rallied, reinforced with Päusch's artillery; the Americans withdrew. Their comrades on the left, after a brisk exchange of fire with Fraser's column, joined a general retreat to the camp on Bemis Heights.

The dangerous & unsoldierly practice of discharging fire Arms [muskets] in camp is possitively prohibited; & any person, except the Savages [Indians] detected in the breach of this Order, is to be immediately stript & recive forty lashes. the Gen¹ calls on every Officer to see this order strictly inforced.—Scandalous & irregular conduct of stragling from camp has prevailed in the army, to the Injury of our cause, & the disgrace of our troops.—to correct such pernitious abuse, (as admonition has failed.) the Gen.¹ finds himself obliged to order every Soldier found beyond the advanced Sentry, unless on command, with an Officer, to be immediately Stript & receive a hundred Lashes. the Commanding Officers of guards are enjoined to see this order punctually Supported.

A GENERAL ORDER TO THE AMERICAN ARMY, FROM THE ORDERLY BOOK OF BRIGADIER GENERAL JOHN GLOVER, DATED SEPTEMBER 27, 1777

Considering the opposing commanders' objectives, the Americans, while losing the battle, had the advantage. Burgoyne possessed the field, but Gates still blocked the route to Albany. Gates' army also suffered fewer casualties in men killed, wounded, and captured in that battle—the Battle of Freeman's Farm; about 300 to Burgoyne's 600.

Neither army made an all-out effort on the 19th. Fraser's men were involved in a limited manner against the Americans' left flank on the battlefield, and would not advance further south toward the American lines, as he did not want to lose contact with the center column. Baron von Riedesel's column was held up in the valley building bridges as they advanced south, and weren't able to get within two miles of the main American lines. Gates

General Sir Henry Clinton

retained approximately 5,000 soldiers, most of whom were Continentals, in the fortifications above the river and on the flats to secure his right flank against any attempt to break through the roadblock.

The soldiers of both armies expected Burgoyne to renew the battle on the 20th. The British commander, however, postponed a second engagement, partly because his hospital was taxed by the large number of wounded. On the morning of the 21st, Burgoyne received a letter from Sir Henry Clinton. He was willing to send 2,000 troops north from the City of New York up through the lower Hudson Highlands if Burgoyne wished him to make such a move. Clinton hoped this move would exert enough pressure south of Albany to make Gates divert troops to cope with the threat. For Burgoyne, the letter was decisive and he decided for certain to wait for this diversion to have its effects before he moved against Gates. In Burgoyne's camp, the rumors were that Clinton was sending a force north to join them and attack Gates' army.

On that same day, within a few hours of Burgoyne's decision to wait for word of Clinton's movements before resuming operation, great cheering and cannon fire were heard from the American camp. Gates' men were celebrating the news that General Lincoln's troops under Colonel Brown had captured Ticonderoga's outworks and taken nearly 300 prisoners. Although the British retained the great fort, as well as Mount Independence, the Americans withdrew to join the operations against Burgoyne. The isolation of the main body of the British army was dramatically demonstrated.

For the next 16 days the armies faced each other, but they were not idle. The British forces constructed a strong fortified line extending in a shallow arc from the Great Redoubt on the bluffs north of the Great Ravine westward to the Freeman farm, where they built a large fort later called the Balcarres

Redoubt. About a quarter of a mile north of that, German troops and American loyalists constructed a log wall called Breymann's Redoubt. The Americans strengthened their own fortifications and collected supplies, while many regiments of militia arrived to augment the army. Gates' men harassed the enemy so relentlessly that Burgoyne issued a new standing order to his army, which commanded his men to form-up with their arms every morning one hour before dawn, so that they could not be so easily surprised by an attack. His troops grew very weary, hungry, and tired.

But all was not well within the American camp. Within three days of the Battle of Freeman's Farm, a dangerous quarrel flared between Gates and Benedict Arnold. Relations between them had so far been cordial, and they had functioned well enough during the critical hours of the 19th when regiments from Arnold's command carried the fight to the British on Freeman's farm. But when Gates prepared his report to Congress, he thanked the officers and men in the units that had fought in the battle with stopping Burgoyne's advance without specifically mentioning Arnold and his division.

The 36-year-old Arnold was not one to take a slight lightly, regardless of the circumstances. He had a reputation for courageous leadership and he was proud of it. He was also a good divisional commander, but

A continental and militia soldier.

In a time when our liberties, lives & everything that is dear is at stake, the Genl. Is sorry to hear jarrings & disputes between the continental troops & the militia lately annexed to his bridage [brigade], which, if incouraged & Continued, must have a tendency to divide & weaken us. For the future he earnestly entreats, & exhorts the commisioned officers of every rank both in the continental & militia regiments to prevent it. Any non commisioned officer or soldier, of either the corps of continental troops, or Militia convicted of abu[s]ive language, or striking each other, will be imediately confined & punished accordingly.

ILLUSTRATION BY ERIC SCHNITZER, SARATOGA NATIONAL HISTORICAL PARK

THE BATTLES OF SARATOGA

General Benedict Arnold

vain, quick-tempered, suspicious, and very sensitive about his "honor" and rank. When Arnold learned of the contents of Gates' report, he interpreted the omission of any reference to his division as a personal affront, a belief in which he was probably encouraged by officers hostile to the northern commander. His anger was fed by a previous general order, given out on the 22nd, making Morgan's corps, which had been posted on the left wing and which Arnold considered part of his division, an independent unit, with its commander responsible directly to Gates.

Never one to suffer silently, Arnold stormed into Gates' quarters and accused the general of insulting him. The two exchanged recriminations, and Arnold threatened to leave the Northern Department. Gates told him that he would be free to go as soon as General Lincoln arrived. Arnold went to his quarters and wrote a long, bitter letter to Gates reviewing his services in the battle of the 19th, reciting his grievances, and demanding a pass to join Washington's army. Gates gave him permission to leave, but it was in the form of a letter that he was to deliver to John Hancock, president of the Continental Congress. Arnold returned the letter, writing to Gates that if he wanted him to deliver the mail, it should be sealed. Gates made out a "common pass" for Arnold to go to Philadelphia. Arnold still refused to leave camp, defied Gates to replace him, and continued to make recommendations concerning the conduct of the campaign. The commanding general had had enough. He gave Lincoln (who had since arrived) command of the right wing, removed Arnold from command, and took over Arnold's division himself. Arnold remained in camp without authority and continued to be the center of a small clique of Schuyler partisans working to discredit Gates for having replaced their former leader.

The situation was dangerous, not only because it threatened the effectiveness of the army's command in the presence of the enemy, but also because it could bring to the surface personal, regional, and social tensions at a time when they might prove fatal to the American cause. That the results were not disastrous was a tribute to the good sense and patriotism of the men and officers in the camp on Bemis Heights.

Meanwhile, the British commander continued to bide his time waiting for news that Clinton was ascending the Hudson. Burgoyne now knew that St. Leger had abandoned the Mohawk expedition and would not meet him in Albany. Cut off from the North, he hoped desperately for succor from the south. Gone were the days when Burgoyne believed that he could accomplish his mission unaided.

Clinton was doing his best to aid Burgoyne, but he was handicapped by a small force and indefinite instructions. When Sir William Howe embarked on his campaign against Philadelphia on July 23, Sir Henry Clinton was left to defend the City of New York with a force of 6,900 infantrymen, of which 3,000 were recently raised loyalist militia. Clinton had disagreed with Howe's plan to attack the American capital, fearing that "Mr. Washington would move with everything he could collect against General Burgoyne or me, and crush the one or the other..." The British position had a perimeter of 100 miles that included large defensive works on three New York islands and the Jersey shore. As long as Washington's army was within striking distance of the city, Clinton could make no move in support of Burgoyne. This was especially true since Major General Israel Putnam commanded about 4,000 Continental and militia troops as well as a small navy in the vicinity of Forts Clinton and Montgomery on the Hudson, about 50 miles north of the City of New York, with orders to guard the Highlands.

Howe was certainly aware of Clinton's predicament and left no instructions to assist Burgoyne by taking the offensive on the lower reaches of the river. At the time, Howe apparently did not anticipate the need for such an offen-

The Genl Positively forbids the troops [from] crouding around the Indian's incampment and recommends it in the strongest manner to the comman[-]ding Officers of Reg.^{TS} to prevent [it] as far as in their lies, every insult offered to the Indians, as the first person detected in abusing them will be severely punished.

A GENERAL ORDER TO THE AMERICAN ARMY, FROM THE ORDERLY BOOK OF BRIGADIER GENERAL JOHN GLOVER, DATED SEPTEMBER 25, 1777

sive. Seven days after setting out on his campaign, however, he had second thoughts and wrote Clinton: "If you can make any diversion in favor of General Burgoyne's approaching Albany, I need not point out the utility of such a measure." Clinton did not consider this a command. Even though the pressure on New York was eased when Washington crossed the Delaware to follow Howe's movements, the New York garrison was still too weak to open the Highlands. Nor was Clinton worried about Burgoyne's situation. He had received a letter written by the northern commander at Fort Edward, just before the Battles of Bennington, which indicated that he expected to reach Albany on about the 23rd of August. Burgoyne made no reference to needing or expecting help from the south.

By the end of August, however, the situation had changed. On September 11, Clinton learned of the British disaster at Bennington and that the army from Canada was still many miles north of its objective. He immediately wrote to Burgoyne: "You know my good-will and are not ignorant of my poverty. If you think 2000 men can assist you effectively, I will make a push at [Fort] Montgomery in about ten days." This was the letter Burgoyne received on the morning of the 21st, convincing him to dig in and wait for help. Burgoyne's reply stated that "an attack or even the menace of an attack upon Fort Montgomery must be of great use, as it will draw away great part of their [Gates'] force...Do it, my dear friend, directly." But the movement upon which Burgoyne came to place so much desperate hope was to be a demonstration only, a limited feint to take pressure off the army from Canada and not a rescue operation. Such a rescue could only be undertaken when expected reinforcements arrived from Europe.

The reinforcements arrived on September 24, about the same time Clinton learned that Washington had withdrawn a part of Putnam's force for service elsewhere. It was now possible for the British to make a move against the Highlands. On the first favorable tide, October 3, Clinton hurried northward with about 3,000 men to attack the Highland forts. By then he knew that Burgoyne's provisions were low and that his communications with Canada had been severed.

The expedition reached Verplanck's Point across the Hudson from Stony Point, on October 5. The small American garrison fled in confusion. While Clinton was preparing to land his troops, an officer arrived from Burgoyne with news that gave a new twist to the situation. The position of the army from Canada was desperate. Losses had reduced it to well below the enemy's strength, and provisions would not last beyond the 20th. Burgoyne claimed that he could force his way to Albany, but was uncertain about supplies when he got there. Before he undertook such a move, he wanted to know if Clinton could open communications and supply him from the south. He asked for explicit orders to attack the enemy on his front or to retreat to Canada.

Clinton, gravely concerned about Burgoyne's situation, resolved to do what he could to relieve the pressure on the army from Canada. At the same time, however, he was irritated by Burgoyne's effort to throw upon him the responsibility of deciding what course to take. In his reply, Clinton declared that he had no orders from Howe relating to Burgoyne's army, that he could not presume to give orders to Burgoyne, who had an independent command, and could do no more than exert pressure on the Americans upon his behalf.

General Putnam's force had been weakened, mostly by having to send detachments to reinforce other armies—the most recent was for Washington after the Battle of Brandywine. He had only about 1,500 Continentals and a few hundred poorly armed militia (many of whom he called "damned unsafe to trust") on both sides of the river. After the Americans evacuated Verplanck's Point, Putnam quickly withdrew four miles into the hills and ordered reinforcements from Forts Clinton and Montgomery to join him. This was precisely the objective that Clinton had intended to achieve by his demonstration at Verplanck's. Leaving about 1,000 men at the Point to mislead Putnam, Clinton crossed to the west bank of the river and marched his infantry through the hills, surprised the two forts, and stormed them with bayonets. The Americans lost both of the forts, a large number of stores, and about half of their 500-man force. The flotilla, guarding obstructions in the river, was unable to escape northward against the wind and was burned or captured.

On October 7 Clinton broke through the log boom the Americans had stretched across the river and routed the small garrison at Fort Constitution near West Point. The next day, he wrote to Burgoyne: "*Nous y voici* and nothing now between us but Gates. I sincerely hope this little success may facilitate your operations... I heartily wish you success." Clinton's message never reached the northern commander. The messenger carrying it was captured and hanged after the note was recovered from a silver bullet he had swallowed. In any case, Clinton's encouraging note would have arrived too late. The day before it was written, Burgoyne had fought his second engagement with Gates—and lost.

Burgoyne knew nothing of Clinton's plans other than the proposed attack on the Highland forts at some future, unspecified date. In his fortified camp at Freeman's farm and the surrounding countryside, Burgoyne decided in early October that he could not wait much longer for the expected relief. Plagued by severe supply shortages, desertions, and faced with advancing autumn, he knew he must act soon. On October 4, the day after his men went on reduced rations and Clinton began his movement northward, Burgoyne called a council of war and made a startling proposal. He would leave 800 men to guard the supplies and use the rest of his army to attack Gates' left and rear. His subordinates were shocked. They argued that it would take too much time to make such a flanking movement; The Americans could overwhelm the 800 men left in camp, seize the supplies, repulse the attack, and cut off the retreat north. The conference adjourned without reaching a decision.

The next day, Baron von Riedesel recommended withdrawing the army to the mouth of the Batten Kill, where communications with the lakes might be reestablished while awaiting news from Clinton. Then, he argued, if no help came from the south, the army would be in a position to retreat. On the face of it, the proposal had merit, but Burgoyne replied that a withdrawal would be disgraceful and futile. The Americans would surely interpret it as a victory, and this, coupled with their numerical and tactical advantages, would give them the psychological incentive to pursue and intercept the Crown forces before they reached a position of safety. Burgoyne was not ready to hazard such a retreat. He was determined to make one more attempt to drive the Americans off Bemis Heights.

He revived his proposal of the 4th in a new form. Instead of committing all but 800 men to a flanking attack, he would organize a reconnaissance-in-force to probe the American left flank and forage for food and supplies in the area near the Americans. If the probing force found conditions favorable, he would then launch an all-out attack on the following day. If an attack were not feasible, he would save his army by withdrawing back to the Batten Kill on the 11th. It was a gamble, but Burgoyne was an old gamester and a proud, brave man who had less fears of fighting against great odds than of being picked to pieces while on the run. His reconnaissance-in-force would move out on October 7.

The reconnaissance force was made up of some of the most elite men

Since it appears that the desertions are increasing, Major General von Riedesel commands that the pickets be increased at six o'clock by as many men as will double the outposts…You must also order the men that one is to keep [a] close watch on each other. Major General von Riedesel promises ten guineas to those who seize their comrades [as they are deserting]. Should it be impossible for a man to have the culprit in his possession, he is permitted to shoot him, and, in the event that he shoots him dead, he will receive five guineas as emolument.

A DIVISIONAL ORDER FOR BARON VON RIEDESEL'S GERMAN TROOPS, FROM THE ORDERLY BOOK OF THE BRUNSWICK CORPS, DATED OCTOBER 2, 1777

drafted from all of the regiments in the army except for the 47th. From Simon Fraser's Advanced Corps came draftees from the British grenadiers, light infantry, and the 24th Regiment. Captain Alexander Fraser's British rangers, Canadian militia, Indians, and loyalists would be sent out through the woods in advance of the reconnaissance force. From Breymann's corps came German jägers, chasseurs, and grenadiers, men who would have been the pride of any European army. Baron von Riedesel's division provided draftees from the Erbprinz, von Riedesel, von Rhetz, and Specht Regiments. Hamilton's division contributed men from the British 9th, 21st, 62nd, and 20th Regiments, most of which bore the heat of battle on September 19. Ten artillery pieces served by more than 100 artillerymen accompanied the column. More than 1,700 officers and men marched out of Fraser's camp, leaving about 5,400 behind to man the fortifications and await the outcome of the probing action.

At about noon, Generals Burgoyne, Phillips, von Riedesel, and Fraser led the men out of camp. They marched south along the Quaker Springs road through the abandoned Coulter farm, woodland, and then into the open fields of the Barber farm. Some Americans were posted there in a house, but the advance guard of the reconnaissance force soon drove them out. Upon entering the field, the British light infantry and the 24th Regiment marched west along a road that cut across the wheatfield, through more woods, and into another, smaller field. There, the light infantry placed itself across this field, at the base of an eminence. The 24th Regiment deployed in the woods on the road that ran through the two fields. The German troops were posted next to them along that same road across the Barber wheatfield, while the British grenadiers formed a line on the Germans' left, mostly in the woods. The detachments of the four regiments from Hamilton's division were to the left of the grenadiers and stretched back toward Freeman's farm. Some of the officers climbed onto the roof of the Barber farmhouse to try to find the American works through a spyglass. The trees in their front, however, were too large to see past. Grain was found in the abandoned field, and word was sent back to camp to have foragers come with wagons to collect it.

The British front, which extended from the field west of the Barber farm to the southern fringe of the Freeman farm, was mostly open, but the British grenadiers and 24 Regiment rested in woods; the light infantry position was overlooked by a great hill. The woods and the hill made the British flanks very vulnerable to an attack. Lieutenant Colonel James Wilkinson, the American deputy adjutant general, observed the force from an American post located south of the Barber farm, and reported the enemy positions to Gates. The commander ordered Morgan's corps and his own left wing to advance and attack the enemy.

Peter Salem at the Battle of Bunker Hill

PETER SALEM WAS ONE OF MANY
AFRICAN-AMERICANS WHO SERVED THE
CAUSE OF AMERICAN INDEPENDENCE.
SALEM'S COMBAT RECORD INCLUDED THE
BATTLE OF BUNKER HILL (PICTURED)
AS WELL AS SARATOGA. THE AMERICAN
ARMY WAS A RACIALLY INTEGRATED
ONE, AND WOULD NOT BE AGAIN
UNTIL THE KOREAN WAR.

COURTESY OF THE CHICAGO HISTORICAL SOCIETY

The main American attack, which opened between 3:30 and 4 p.m., was classic in its direct simplicity. Poor's brigade attacked the left, where the British grenadiers and the units from Hamilton's division stood. Colonel Morgan's corps of riflemen and light infantry struck the enemy's right, composed of the British light infantry and the 24th Regiment. Learned's target was the Germans in the center of the line.

Poor's men soon overwhelmed the greatly outnumbered grenadiers, whose commander, Major John Dyke Acland, fell after he was shot through both legs and was captured. They then struck Hamilton's men, who were strung out in a thin line from the Quaker Springs road to near the southern end of the Balcarres Redoubt. Morgan's corps opened fire on the British light infantry in their clearing west of the Barber farm, and Fraser's veterans began falling before the deadly accuracy of the Pennsylvania and Virginia riflemen. Dearborn's American light infantry rushed at the British light infantry with their bayonets, forcing them to fall back toward the woods. Despite the soldiers' dogged courage and the skill of their officers, Fraser's men were forced to withdraw behind the Germans and were deployed across the road to Quaker

General Simon Fraser

(1729-1777) COMMANDED
THE ADVANCED CORPS OF
GENERAL BURGOYNE'S ARMY.
FRASER'S MORTAL WOUNDING
ON OCTOBER 7 DEPRIVED
THE BRITISH ARMY OF ONE
OF ITS ABLEST LEADERS.

SARATOGA NATIONAL HISTORICAL PARK

Springs. As Morgan's corps rolled back the British right, Fraser rode among his men, encouraging and rallying them to maintain their ranks, keep up their fire, and make the Americans pay dearly for every foot of ground. He knew that he had to preserve the right flank long enough to allow the center and the remnants of the left to make an orderly withdrawal. But the Scotsman's efforts were in vain. He could not stop the turning movement. As Simon Fraser made his stand near the road, he was targeted by many sharpshooters and wounded mortally. He was hurriedly carried off the field back to the British camp. His command passed to a fellow Scot and commander of the British light infantry, Lord Balcarres.

While Morgan and Poor drove back the enemy's flanks, Learned's brigade, soon supported by Brigadier General Abraham Ten Broeck's brigade of New York militia and a regiment from Jonathan Warner's brigade of Massachusetts militia, struck the Germans, who, with both flanks exposed, stubbornly fought them off. In the midst of the attack, Benedict Arnold rode onto the field and, though he had no command, led another assault that caused the Germans to join the general retreat into the Balcarres Redoubt.

By 5 p.m. the probing column had lost eight cannons and suffered more than 400 casualties. Burgoyne's plan was thwarted, but behind the strong walls of the Balcarres Redoubt his soldiers were still capable of putting up a stiff fight, as Poor's men soon discovered. After the Germans were routed, Arnold left Learned's troops and joined Poor's. Through the woods behind the Coulter and Freeman farms, Poor's men pursued the retreating enemy. They poured over the "Bloody Knoll," so-called for the heavy casualties there, overran its small outpost, and swarmed into the open ground in front of the Balcarres Redoubt. A withering fire met them as they charged. Poor soon realized that they were against odds too great, and his brigade eventually moved back under cover, continuing to skirmish with the ominous redoubt before them.

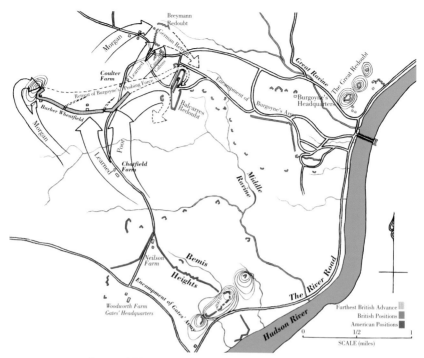

Second Battle of Saratoga: Bemis Heights

OCTOBER 7, 1777

MAP BY ERIC SCHNITZER, SARATOGA NATIONAL HISTORICAL PARK

While the remnants of Burgoyne's reconnaissance force were retreating into the Balcarres Redoubt, fresh American troops from Bemis Heights began to move toward the sounds of battle. Paterson's brigade, one of Brigadier General John Glover's regiments, and the 5th and 6th Massachusetts Regiments from Brigadier General John Nixon's brigade brought the number of Americans moving toward the fields of battle or engaged in actual fighting to nearly 7,000.

While Poor's men fought and died in front of the strongest British position, Morgan's men, reinforced by regiments from Learned's brigade, deployed to attack the northern right flank of Burgoyne's camp, consisting of more than 150 German grenadiers, chasseurs, and artillerymen in the Breymann Redoubt. The two companies of Canadian militia, which were charged with defending the two log cabins located between the Breymann Redoubt and the Balcarres Redoubt, had not returned from the expedition—

Boot Monument

the cabins were virtually undefended. Because the Breymann Redoubt was backed only by a small camp and woods, its left and rear was now exposed. The Americans mounted a massive attack on the Germans. While most of the men stormed the front of the redoubt, a part of Learned's command and some riflemen swept through the gap left by the Canadians and into the Germans' rear. Arnold, who had heard the firing on his left, abandoned Poor's troops and joined the Americans attacking the rear of the Breymann Redoubt. Colonel Breymann fell dead, and the German defense collapsed. Arnold suffered a severe leg wound (now memorialized by the famous Arnold "Boot Monument" on the battlefield). The redoubt and Breymann's camp were captured, as were its two 6-pound cannons, and set on fire.

Possession of the Breymann Redoubt opened the right and rear of Burgoyne's camp to the Americans. A desperate effort made by about 50 Germans attempting to recapture the fortification failed. Their leader, Lieutenant Colonel Ernst Ludwig Wilhelm von Speth, was captured with a few others; the rest took for the woods. As darkness ended the day's fighting, the British situation was desperate; the army lay in an indefensible position in the presence of a numerically superior enemy. Leaving their campfires burning, the soldiers of the Royal Army withdrew under cover of darkness to the heights of the Great Redoubt over-

Burial of General Fraser

OCTOBER 8, 1777. HAVING REQUESTED A SIMPLE BURIAL, SIMON
FRASER'S REMAINS WERE INTERRED WITH A MINIMUM OF POMP.
NONETHELESS, BURGOYNE AND THE ARMY'S SENIOR OFFICERS ATTENDED
FRASER'S BURIAL. ARGUABLY, THE DELAY CAUSED BY THE BURIAL
SERVICE COST BURGOYNE IRREPLACEABLE TIME TO MAKE A
SUCCESSFUL RETREAT.

SARATOGA NATIONAL HISTORICAL PARK

looking the river road. Along that road also lay their hospital, artillery park, and supply depot.

All the next day, Burgoyne's weary, badly mauled men rested in a strong position. The Americans occupied the former British camp and kept up a steady cannonade, and American patrols were sent out to reconnoiter the new positions of the enemy. General Benjamin Lincoln himself went out on such a reconnaissance and mistakenly "fell in with a body of the enemy's troops." As many of the troops were wearing blue-colored coats, Lincoln mistook them for his own. However, as he approached them, he realized his mistake—they were German soldiers. They turned to fire upon him, and like Arnold the day before, he was severely wounded in the leg. Gates would have to manage his whole army without the help of a major general.

Shortly before sunset on that same day, a party of British and German officers slowly ascended the largest hill of the Great Redoubt, bearing the body of Simon Fraser to his grave. As the Royal Artillery Chaplain, Edward Brudenell, intoned the Church of England's solemn Burial Office, American cannons made even that duty hazardous.

The time had come when Burgoyne must make a decision he dreaded more than battle. He had been decisively defeated in the field and only the rapid evacuation of his fortified camp to a strong temporary position had saved his army. He faced two alternatives: surrender or retreat. His pride and the fading, desperate hope that he could still profit from an aggressive move by Clinton persuaded him to try to buy time by retreating. If all else failed, perhaps the Americans might yet commit some tactical blunder that would permit him to escape. The old gambler was still fighting the odds.

Gates had accomplished his primary goal of stopping the British advance; now he had an opportunity to capture Burgoyne's whole army. He had always appreciated the necessity of denying his opponent access to the north and east and had done everything in his power to accomplish that end. Fortunately for the Americans, their growing numerical strength gave Gates enough manpower to isolate Burgoyne from his northern bases. During the first week of October, he posted militia on the east bank of the Hudson in the enemy's rear and received reinforcements from several areas. Stark and his militia reappeared, captured the small garrison at Fort Edward, and moved down along the river toward Saratoga. More Vermonters under Brigadier General Jacob Bailey occupied an entrenched position along the road that ran north of Fort Edward. Brigadier General John Fellows with a brigade of Massachusetts militia moved up the east side of the Hudson, crossed the river, and began to entrench at Saratoga. Thus, when Burgoyne decided to retreat, there was a growing number of American soldiers behind him and more than 12,000 in front of him. He summed up the situation with these words: "A defeated army was to retreat from an enemy flushed with success, much superior in front and occupying strong posts in the country behind. We were equally liable upon that march to be attacked in the front, flank, or rear."

Beginning in the afternoon of the 8th, Burgoyne's army began its retreat northward. It was a slow process, especially with the artillery and baggage in tow. The Advanced Corps, led by Lord Balcarres, formed the rear guard of the withdrawal, and left well into the early morning hours of the next day. About 400 of Burgoyne's wounded and sick were left behind in the hospital, with a letter written by Burgoyne requesting that Gates protect them. Burgoyne's army slogged through a cold, dark autumn downpour toward Saratoga, while the whole army of men, women, and children had to endure many tense halts along the way for reasons left unknown even to the officers. In Saratoga, eight miles north of where the two battles had taken place, Fellows'

Massachusetts militia barred the way to the river crossing. Lieutenant Colonel Nicholas Sutherland of the 47th Regiment urged Burgoyne to let him attack the Americans, whose security was temptingly lax. Because the regiment could muster only 250 men to attack Fellows' 1,300 in a prepared position, Burgoyne decided that the odds were too great and refused to grant the colonel's request. Instead, he kept his troops together as he approached Saratoga. Fellows did not wait for the British to attack; he withdrew across the river and entrenched along the crest of the hills, covering the ford over which the road crossed.

While Burgoyne's men dragged themselves northward, Gates' soldiers drew and cooked rations, replenished their ammunition, and prepared to pursue the enemy. Once under way, Gates' army marched northward with dispatch, following Burgoyne's line of retreat. While the cold rains of the 9th had made Burgoyne's retreat slow and miserable, Gates' army set out after them early the next day under more favorable conditions.

The American advance guards reached the Fish Kill in the early afternoon of the 10th and found the enemy encamped on the heights of Saratoga north of the creek. Upon hearing that the Americans were advancing, the British that very morning burned the mills, outbuildings, and main house of Philip Schuyler's country estate to prevent Gates' soldiers from using them for cover.

If the opposing armies had been approximately equal, Burgoyne's position would have been strong. Just north of the Fish Kill a ridge stretches northward, breaks sharply to the east, and flattens into a plateau to the west. The soldiers threw up entrenchments along this ridge, working feverishly from the chill fall mornings until past the early dusk under constant fire from American artillery and small arms. Despite the recent defeat, short rations, and physical privation and discomfort, they were still capable of putting up a defense that would do honor to reputations won on European battlefields.

The main body of Gates' army reached the south side of the Fish Kill at Saratoga in the late afternoon of the 10th. Major Ebenezer Stevens, commander of the American artillery, immediately placed his cannons on the flats south of the Fish Kill near General Schuyler's smoldering estate and opened fire on the British batteaux and working parties near the river. Earlier that same day, Burgoyne had sent the 47th Regiment, Fraser's British rangers, MacKay's company of loyalists, and the artificers north along the road that ran west of the river to a crossing near Fort Edward, in order to repair bridges and scout the area. The British troops were later recalled in anticipation of an attack on Saratoga by Gates' army, as the Americans began to show themselves in force. The rest of the now even smaller detachment was attacked by militia and fled.

When reports of the road repair party moving out of the British camp

Lady Christian Harriet Acland

reached Gates, he was convinced that the enemy was evacuating and leaving only a small rear-guard behind. Gates then ordered Nixon's brigade to advance the next morning, on the 11th, to be followed by other brigades of the army. As the Americans advanced for an attack, a British soldier, who was deserting at that very moment, warned Brigadier General John Glover that Burgoyne's army had not left. Learned's brigade and Morgan's corps, also sent out to attack, met with unexpected resistance in the morning fog. When the tip was confirmed, and it became apparent that Burgoyne's troops were still in position and prepared to defend themselves, the Americans broke contact, began to surround the encampment, and settled down to what amounted to a siege of the position.

Gates was under pressure from some of his staff and civil leaders in Albany to attack Burgoyne's camp and bring the campaign to an immediate close. Some of the more impetuous officers were eager to add luster to their laurels by attacking an enemy whose weakness seemed to guarantee an easy victory. More responsible men believed that an attack should be made for other reasons. Of the 12,500 men present and fit for duty in the army under the direct command of Gates, nearly half were supporting militia. A reported 4,500 more militia troops were acting in cooperation with Gates, and made up separate armies to the north and east of Burgoyne. When their terms of service expired, these men would probably go home, as Colonel Ezra May's 2nd Hampshire County Regiment of Massachusetts militia had done on October 14. While it was true that the Americans outnumbered Burgoyne's troops by more than two to one, many of the militia, because of their inexperience and more democratic disposition, were of limited value. Nevertheless, their presence helped give the Americans a comforting sense of superiority, while impressing upon the enemy a feeling of despair. Another factor, especially among the civilians, was concern about Clinton's operations. If that threat grew and materialized, and if the militia departed, the opportunity to destroy Burgoyne might be lost.

Clinton's activities were in everyone's thoughts—giving Burgoyne his last, desperate hope of salvation and disturbing Gates' peace of mind. Clinton had no intention of moving on Albany after taking the Highland forts, but neither commander at Saratoga knew that; and the events taking place after the capture of those works gave color to the belief that Clinton had more ambitious purposes in mind. On October 13, he ordered Major General John Vaughan with 1,700 men, supported by a flotilla under Captain Sir James Wallace, "to feel his way to General Burgoyne and do his utmost to assist his operation or even to join him if required." Vaughan and Wallace burned Esopus (now Kingston, NY) on the 16th and moved up-river to Livingston Manor, about 45 miles south of Albany. They got no further. At Vaughan's approach, civilian leaders in Albany importuned Gates to reinforce General Putnam's troops defending the approach to Albany from the south. Gates responded by sending them soldiers from Fort Stanwix and more than 500 men from General Ten Broeck's militia brigade from his own army. Hundreds more militia were ordered out, and much of the countryside rallied to the call to arms. When the British reached Livingston Manor they found Americans blocking their path. Vaughan notified Clinton that he could not get through to Burgoyne, since there were now 6,500 American troops facing him. In the meantime, Clinton had received orders from General Howe, who had run into more opposition than expected in Pennsylvania, to send reinforcements to Philadelphia. Vaughan was ordered to withdraw.

Burgoyne, who knew much less about what was happening to the south than did Gates, clung to his hopes. But as the days passed, those hopes were more difficult to sustain in the face of the knowledge that rations would be exhausted soon, that getting drinking water from the river or the Fish Kill was too dangerous due to American patrols and snipers, and that many of the soldiers were without shelter and under the constant fire from an increasingly stronger American army.

Burgoyne convened a council of war with most of his general officers on October 12. He reviewed the situation in starkly realistic detail, and requested the opinions of his generals on the following propositions: (1) to await an attack; (2) to attack the enemy; (3) to retreat with artillery and baggage; (4) to retreat at night without artillery and baggage; (5) to march rapidly to Albany if the enemy, by extending to his left, should leave his rear open. General von Riedesel insisted that the fourth proposition was the only practical one, but it was eliminated when a reconnaissance revealed that it would be impossible to accomplish with secrecy, due to the presence of American militia north and east of them.

Another council met at 3 p.m. on the 13th, and the members decided that their situation justified the seeking of honorable terms for a capitulation. Burgoyne had already prepared the articles of a treaty before the council met, to which his attending officers unanimously approved, and negotiations were begun on the morning of the 14th at Gates' headquarters. During the discussion, the American commander presented to Lieutenant Colonel Robert Kingston, Burgoyne's representative and aide-de-camp, terms for unconditional surrender. Burgoyne and his officers rejected them, saying they "would rather die" than accept Gates' demands. The British commander then presented his own terms. To everyone's surprise, Gates agreed to most of the details with the stipulation that the capitulation must be accomplished by 2 o'clock that afternoon (the 15th). Burgoyne grew suspicious and quickly surmised that Gates' sudden eagerness to conclude negotiations must mean that Clinton's expedition was approaching Albany.

If this were true, Burgoyne knew that his wisest course would be to delay negotiations long enough for Clinton to come to his relief or bring sufficient pressure on the Americans to force Gates to raise the siege. He convened another council, which decided to inform the American commander that, while the basis of the treaty was agreed to, the British needed more time to study some minor matters. Burgoyne proposed to have two commissioners from each army meet to resolve the differences in terms.

The commissioners met on the late afternoon of the 15th on General Schuyler's property just south of the Fish Kill. After lengthy discussion, they signed the articles of capitulation. Burgoyne's officers demurred at the term "capitulation," and the "Articles of Capitulation" became the "Articles of Convention." Gates hoped that this concession, which he did not feel to be important except to the defeated enemy's pride, would bring the negotiations to a close.

His hopes were premature. A loyalist came into Burgoyne's camp on the night of the 15th and told him that Clinton had advanced to Esopus nearly a week ago—an event to which he admitted having no firsthand account of. Unaware that Vaughan had stopped south of Albany, the British commander called another council and asked his officers two questions: could he honorably break the convention, and if the fragmentary and vague news of Clinton's operations to the south were true, did this improve their situation? On a vote, a majority of the officers answered negatively to both questions. Burgoyne continued to play for time. He wrote another letter to Gates accusing him of sending a sizable detachment of troops to Albany during the negotiations, which had reduced the numerical superiority that had initially prompted Burgoyne to negotiate, and therefore nullified the convention. To confirm this, Burgoyne requested that two British officers be permitted to check on the American strength. Gates rejected Burgoyne's reasoning and said that such a request was "inadmissible," that it was up to Burgoyne to ratify or dissolve the treaty, and that he expected an immediate and decisive reply. After another council of war, the British commander signed the "Convention of Saratoga" on the 16th, acknowledging defeat and delivering up his army to the Americans.

The surrender took place on October 17, 1777. The day dawned clear and cool, and the forests of the northern Hudson Valley were at the height of their autumnal splendor when Gates' soldiers paraded on the river road south of the Fish Kill. Most of them were not in uniform, but several of Burgoyne's officers testified to their good physical condition and soldierly bearing. These men had earned a respected place in history reserved for few others. They had defeated a brave, well-trained, professionally led army, and they were about to witness the first surrender of a British army on American soil.

At the appointed hour, Burgoyne, his general officers, and their staffs rode across the ford, between the American soldiers drawn up on both sides of the road, and past the colonial Dutch Reformed Church to Gates' headquarters. Meanwhile, north of the creek, near the remains of Fort Hardy, the men who had fought faithfully against great odds laid down their arms, some with grim dignity, others with obvious grief and resentment. They too crossed the ford,

Articles of Convention

SARATOGA NATIONAL HISTORIC PARK

Surrender of John Burgoyne.

past the silent lines of victorious Americans. In the presence of both armies, Burgoyne tendered his sword to the American general who had once been a British major. Gates returned the sword. While the "Convention Army" marched away to captivity, the principal officers on both sides retired to Gates' marquee to dine.

The terms of the convention stipulated that Burgoyne's army would be returned to Europe, but because this would have freed other units to fight in America, the Continental Congress interposed a succession of objections and those terms were never honored. The Convention Army was taken first to Cambridge, Massachusetts and put into huts located on Winter Hill and Prospect Hill. General Burgoyne returned to England on parole the next year and many other officers were exchanged, but the army was moved to Rutland, Massachusetts in 1778. They began another move in November, this time to Virginia, and were eventually barracked near Charlottesville in January of 1779. After living there for over a year, the Convention Army was dispersed to various places and interned for the duration of the war. Many of the soldiers of the Convention Army remained in America—permanently.

Fruits of Victory

The Convention of Saratoga took one of Britain's armies out of the war, and with it went her prospects of bringing the conflict to an early end through major land campaigns. Gone were the ill-defined hopes of Burgoyne, Howe, and the Cabinet for a victory in 1777 by capturing the American capital city of Philadelphia, invading the northern interior, and somehow uniting the two British armies to crush the rebellion. The king's ministers and generals reassessed the task in America and shifted their strategy to an emphasis on naval warfare and the capture of more limited strategic targets. The center of the war moved to the sea and the South, and the conflict in the North stalemated while the British undertook a war of attrition aimed at eroding the American will to fight.

The British achieved only one of the goals for 1777: Sir William Howe's capture of Philadelphia. But that success was made hollow by the failure of the northern campaign and the fruits of that failure. British plans suffered for the lack of a unifying concept. They rested upon the reckless premise that Howe could safely operate in Pennsylvania while a substantial garrison was immobilized on Manhattan and while Burgoyne was left to his own devices, each isolated from the others. The two campaigns were developed independently by Howe in New York and Burgoyne in England. They were out of contact with one another and gave almost no thought to what should have been their major concern—how to coordinate their offensives. But both men focused almost exclusively on his own undertaking, and the two plans were as different as their creators.

Burgoyne's plan called for speed and audacity in moving a relatively small force (by European standards) along a predetermined route to a goal that was not clearly defined; the terms "cooperation" and "communication" could be, and were in many instances, interpreted differently by their author, Burgoyne, and by Howe, Clinton, and Germain. Howe's plan called for deliberately moving a large army to a fixed geographical and political objective by a route that was not agreed upon until the last possible moment. Burgoyne was absorbed with reaching Albany and not with what might happen after he got there, beyond vaguely expecting to open communications and cooperate with Howe. Howe was obsessed with capturing Philadelphia and not with what might happen on the Hudson or how he would employ the troops from Canada once they reached Albany.

Because war narrows the perspective of field commanders, they frequently suffer from "occupational myopia." But they are not sovereign. Government is responsible, theoretically at least, for seeing the whole picture and planning accordingly—assigning priorities, allocating resources, and requiring its military servants to integrate their efforts. This responsibility rested with the Cabinet in general and Germain in particular. The colonial secretary failed to discharge that responsibility. He knew that Howe intended to go to Pennsylvania. Despite warnings from Clinton, the lack of coordination between Burgoyne and Howe did not concern Germain early enough to make him effective in imposing unity on their campaigns.

Germain failed to explain Burgoyne's mission to Howe, contenting himself with sending that commander a copy of the letter to Carleton that contained Burgoyne's instructions. He did not raise the subject of an integrated effort with Howe until the middle of May, and then it was too late. By the time Howe received Germain's letter, he was already on his way to Philadelphia. Contrary to a persistent tradition, there were no "lost orders" directing Howe to ascend the Hudson; such orders never existed. Germain was confident that the two armies could shift for themselves until autumn and then, with Albany and Philadelphia secured, somehow establish contact and coordinate their future moves.

Despite the defects in British planning, the Americans did not win by default. While under the command of Philip Schuyler they slowed Burgoyne's advance, and their successes at Bennington and Fort Stanwix certainly contributed to the victory at Saratoga. But, Burgoyne might still have reached Albany if it had not been for the sound strategy that Horatio Gates developed after he took command of the Northern Department. He husbanded his resources and built up an overwhelming force that gave him the flexibility required to cope with Burgoyne's threat by isolating him and forcing him to fight on American terms. That strategy was ably executed by the army's general officers and regimental commanders. Finally, the Americans' great numerical superiority enabled them to defeat the soldiers of the Royal Army in two engagements that were largely fought according to standard European practices.

Saratoga was not a victory of frontier tactics over those of the Old World. Both armies had light troops that used concealment and marksmanship in a manner dear to the imagination of romantics. Morgan's riflemen, Dearborn's light infantrymen, and their Iroquois and Stockbridge Indian warrior allies had their counterparts in the British rangers, Lord Balcarres' light infantry, German chasseurs and jägers, and their Iroquois and Algonquian warrior allies. However, the brunt of the fight was borne by the majority of regiments in both armies who deployed and fought in line, firing by volley in the manner that made their short-range muskets effective.

The Americans' victory at Saratoga boosted their morale and profoundly affected their military fortunes by internationalizing the war. After months

Capitulacion du Burgoyne

of covertly supporting the Americans, while weighing the pros and cons of becoming a belligerent, France's drift toward open involvement in the American conflict had reached a point by September 1777 where she was about to go to war against her ancient rival. The Declaration of Independence and the Americans' refusal to renounce that document as a condition for peace had, for the time being at least, ruled out the probability of a reconciliation between Britain and the rebellious colonies. The question of whether the Americans would be effective military allies had to be answered.

Despite the fall of Philadelphia, the French were encouraged by Howe's failure to destroy Washington's army in Pennsylvania, and they were especially impressed by the American commander-in-chief's audacity in the Battle of Germantown. Further encouragement came from a favorable report on the condition and morale of the Continental Army submitted by Johann de Kalb, a German who on September 15, 1777 became a major general in the American army. Gates' victory at Saratoga was even more persuasive proof that the Americans could and would fight.

Soon after receiving news of the American success at Saratoga, the French government decided that it was time to join the rebels in their fight against Great Britain. On January 8, 1778, the French foreign minister, Comte de Vergennes, notified Benjamin Franklin, Silas Deane, and Arthur Lee, the American envoys in Paris, that his government was prepared to enter into an alliance. On February 6, the three American representatives and Conrad Alexandre Gerard, France's minister to the United States, signed a treaty of amity and commerce recognizing American independence. This was followed that same day by a treaty of alliance that brought France into the war as an active belligerent. In 1779, Spain, France's ally, declared war on England. The American Revolution had ceased being merely a family fight; it had become an international war. French and Spanish credits, money, supplies, ships, and men, without which American success would have been in doubt, supported the United States and helped to pave the way to victory on October 19, 1781, when Lieutenant General Charles Lord Cornwallis surrendered to a Franco-American army at Yorktown, Virginia. Saratoga had borne great fruit.

Appendices

1. ORGANIZATION OF THE ARMY UNDER THE COMMAND OF MAJOR GENERAL HORATIO GATES AT BEMIS HEIGHTS ON SEPTEMBER 19, 1777

The Left Wing

(also called "Arnold's division") commanded by Major General Benedict Arnold

Benedict Arnold's general staff [1]

Morgan's Corps, commanded by Colonel Daniel Morgan
Battalion of Riflemen (the Rifle Regiment), Colonel Daniel Morgan [2]
Light Infantry Battalion, Major Henry Dearborn [3]

Poor's Brigade, commanded by Brigadier General Enoch Poor
1st New Hampshire Regiment, Colonel Joseph Cilley
2nd New Hampshire Regiment, Lieutenant Colonel Winborn Adams
3rd New Hampshire Regiment, Colonel Alexander Scammell
2nd New York Regiment, Colonel Philip Van Cortlandt
4th New York Regiment, Colonel Henry Beekman Livingston
Regiment of Connecticut militia, Colonel Thaddeus Cook
Regiment of Connecticut militia, Colonel Jonathan Lattimer

Learned's Brigade, commanded by Brigadier General Ebenezer Learned
2nd Massachusetts Regiment, Colonel John Bailey
8th Massachusetts Regiment, Lieutenant Colonel John Brooks
9th Massachusetts Regiment, Colonel James Wesson
1st Canadian Regiment (Livingston's New York Regiment),
Colonel James Livingston

The Right Wing

(also called "Gates' division") commanded by Major General Horatio Gates

Horatio Gates' headquarters staff

Paterson's Brigade, commanded by Brigadier General John Paterson
10th Massachusetts Regiment, Colonel Thomas Marshall
11th Massachusetts Regiment, Colonel Benjamin Tupper
12th Massachusetts Regiment, Colonel Samuel Brewer
14th Massachusetts Regiment, Colonel Gamaliel Bradford

Nixon's Brigade, commanded by Brigadier General John Nixon
3rd Massachusetts Regiment, Colonel John Greaton
5th Massachusetts Regiment, Colonel Rufus Putnam
6th Massachusetts Regiment, Colonel Thomas Nixon
7th Massachusetts Regiment, Lieutenant Colonel William Stacey

Glover's Brigade, commanded by Brigadier General John Glover
1st Massachusetts Regiment, Colonel Joseph Vose
4th Massachusetts Regiment, Colonel William Shepard
13th Massachusetts Regiment, Colonel Edward Wigglesworth
15th Massachusetts Regiment, Lieutenant Colonel Henry Haskell
Battalion of Albany County, New York militia, Colonel Abraham Wemple [4]
Battalion of Albany County, New York militia, Colonel William Whiting [4]
Battalion of Dutchess and Ulster County, New York militia,
Colonel Morris Graham [5]

Attached to the Army

Engineer's Department, Colonel Jeduthan Baldwin
Quartermaster Department, Colonel Morgan Lewis
Hospital Department, Doctor Jonathan Potts
commissary departments
wagon-men, batteaux-men
camp followers

Cavalry

2nd Troop, 2nd Continental Dragoons, Captain Jean Louis de Vernejoux
2nd Regiment of Connecticut Light Horse, Major Elijah Hyde

Artillery, commanded by Major Ebenezer Stevens [6]
Stevens' Provisional Artillery Battalion, consisting of one 9-pounder, four 6-pounders, fifteen 4-pounders, and two 3-pounders

1. A general's staff includes both personal and command support personnel needed to help the general manage the command under his direction.
2. This detachment joined the Northern Department on September 3. It was a temporary unit, sent by Washington, to act as a "countenance to the Indians." The men were drafted from the 3rd and 11th Virginia regiments, the 8th Pennsylvania Regiment, as well as other Continental regiments from Virginia, Pennsylvania, and Maryland. They were disbanded at Valley Forge, and ordered back to their parent units.
3. Dearborn was appointed to command the 300-man light infantry battalion, divided into five companies, which was formed by draftees from "the Several Regements in the Northern Army" on September 11, 1777.
4. Governor George Clinton wrote to General Abraham Ten Broeck on August 1 about the necessity of calling out the militia to stop Burgoyne's advance. Clinton ordered two battalions to be formed, commanded by Colonel Abraham Wemple (of the 2nd Albany County militia) and Colonel William Whiting (of the 17th Albany County militia). These two battalions were called "the First Regiment" and "the Second Regiment" respectively. They were made up of draftees from Albany County militia regiments, and were to serve as such until November 15.
5. Governor George Clinton also wrote to Colonel Morris Graham on August 1 about the necessity of calling out the militia to stop Burgoyne's advance. Draftees from Colonel Frear's (4th Regiment), Colonel Humfrey's (5th Regiment) Colonel Sutherland's, and Graham's 6th Regiment of Dutchess County, as well as Colonel Snyder's

(1st Regiment), and Colonel Pawling's (3rd Regiment) from Ulster County, NY were to form a battalion to be put "under the Command of his Hnor., Major General Schuyler." The battalion was to be commanded by Colonel Graham, and the men "drafted by ballot or other equitable manner." They were ordered to serve until November 1.

6. Ebenezer Stevens, commander of this artillery battalion, was breveted to the rank of major in the Continental Army in May, and the battalion was considered a detachment of the Continental artillery. This battalion, which had a company of artillery artificers, became part of the 3rd Continental Artillery Regiment in 1778.

2. ORGANIZATION OF THE ARMY UNDER THE COMMAND OF MAJOR GENERAL HORATIO GATES AT BEMIS HEIGHTS ON OCTOBER 7, 1777

Morgan's Corps, commanded by Colonel Daniel Morgan
Battalion of Riflemen (the Rifle Regiment), Colonel Daniel Morgan
Light Infantry Battalion, Lieutenant Colonel Henry Dearborn

The Left Wing

commanded by Major General Horatio Gates
Horatio Gates' headquarters staff

Poor's Brigade, commanded by Brigadier General Enoch Poor
1st New Hampshire Regiment, Colonel Joseph Cilley
2nd New Hampshire Regiment, Lieutenant Colonel Jeremiah Gilman
3rd New Hampshire Regiment, Colonel Alexander Scammell
2nd New York Regiment, Colonel Philip Van Cortlandt
4th New York Regiment, Colonel Henry Beekman Livingston
Regiment of Connecticut militia, Colonel Thaddeus Cook
Regiment of Connecticut militia, Colonel Jonathan Lattimer

Learned's Brigade, commanded by Brigadier General Ebenezer Learned
2nd Massachusetts Regiment, Colonel John Bailey
8th Massachusetts Regiment, Lieutenant Colonel John Brooks
9th Massachusetts Regiment, Colonel James Wesson
1st Canadian Regiment (Livingston's New York Regiment),
Colonel James Livingston
Regiment of New Hampshire militia, Colonel Stephen Evans [1]
Regiment of New Hampshire militia, Colonel Abraham Drake [1]

Ten Broeck's Brigade (also called "Schuyler's brigade"),
consisting of militia detachments from New York's Albany County,
commanded by Brigadier General Abraham Ten Broeck [2]
1st Regiment, Colonel Jacob Lansing Jr.
2nd Regiment, Major Abraham Swits
3rd Regiment, Colonel Philip P. Schuyler
4th Regiment, Colonel Robert Killian Van Rensselaer
5th Regiment, Colonel Gerrit G. Van den Bergh
6th Regiment, Colonel Stephen John Schuyler
7th Regiment, Colonel Abraham Van Alstine
8th Regiment, Colonel Robert Van Rensselaer
9th Regiment, Colonel Peter Van Ness
10th Regiment, Colonel Henry Livingston
11th Regiment, Colonel Anthony Van Bergen
12th Regiment, Colonel Jacobus Van Schoonhoven
13th Regiment, Colonel John McCrea
14th Regiment, Colonel John Knickerbacker
16th Regiment, Colonel Lewis Van Woert
17th Regiment, Lieutenant Colonel Asa Waterman

The Right Wing

commanded by Major General Benjamin Lincoln [3]

Benjamin Lincoln's general staff

Paterson's Brigade, commanded by Brigadier General John Paterson
10th Massachusetts Regiment, Colonel Thomas Marshall
11th Massachusetts Regiment, Colonel Benjamin Tupper
12th Massachusetts Regiment, Colonel Samuel Brewer
14th Massachusetts Regiment, Colonel Gamaliel Bradford
1st [South] Berkshire County Regiment, Massachusetts militia,
Colonel John Ashley [4]
3rd York County Regiment, Massachusetts militia, Lieutenant
Colonel Joseph Storer [4]

Nixon's Brigade, commanded by Brigadier General John Nixon
3rd Massachusetts Regiment, Colonel John Greaton
5th Massachusetts Regiment, Colonel Rufus Putnam
6th Massachusetts Regiment, Colonel Thomas Nixon
7th Massachusetts Regiment, Colonel Ichabod Alden
2nd Hampshire County Regiment, Massachusetts militia,
Colonel Ezra May [5]

Glover's Brigade, commanded by Brigadier General John Glover
1st Massachusetts Regiment, Colonel Joseph Vose
4th Massachusetts Regiment, Colonel William Shepard
13th Massachusetts Regiment, Colonel Edward Wigglesworth
15th Massachusetts Regiment, Colonel Timothy Bigelow

Battalion of Albany County, New York militia, Colonel Abraham Wemple
Battalion of Albany County, New York militia, Colonel William Whiting
Battalion of Dutchess and Ulster County, New York militia,
Colonel Morris Graham

Warner's Brigade, commanded by Brigadier General Jonathan Warner [6]
Central Berkshire County Regiment, Massachusetts militia,
Colonel John Brown
5th Middlesex County Regiment, Massachusetts militia,
Colonel Samuel Bullard
3rd Suffolk County Regiment, Massachusetts militia, Colonel Benjamin Gill
1st Hampshire County Regiment, Massachusetts militia, Colonel Benjamin Woodbridge
4th Essex County Regiment, Massachusetts militia, Colonel Samuel Johnson

Attached to the Army

Battalion of Connecticut militia, Brigadier General Oliver Wolcott [7]
Iroquois Indian warriors [8]
Stockbridge Indians [9]
Engineer's Department, Colonel Jeduthan Baldwin
Quartermaster Department, Colonel Morgan Lewis
Hospital Department, Doctor Jonathan Potts
commissary departments
wagon-men, batteaux-men
camp followers

Cavalry

2nd Troop, 2nd Continental Dragoons, Captain Jean Louis de Vernejoux [10]
2nd Regiment of Connecticut Light Horse, Major Elijah Hyde

Artillery, commanded by Major Ebenezer Stevens
Stevens' Provisional Artillery Battalion, consisting of one 9-pounder, four 6-pounders, fifteen 4-pounders, and two 3-pounders

1. These regiments arrived on October 7.
2. These militia regiments were not called out until September 18. They would "trickle in," but most would be present by October 4. The governor did not call out Colonel Peter Vroman's 15th Albany County Militia Regiment, as they had duties in the Schoharie Valley.
3. He assumed command of the right wing of the army on September 25.
4. These regiments were present by October 2.
5. This regiment arrived on October 4, "remained in camp" on October 7, and "went home" October 14.
6. This brigade arrived on September 24.
7. This battalion was present by October 4.
8. Philip Schuyler wrote to Gates from Albany on September 15 that "some of the Oenidas, Tuscarroras and Onondagoes have arrived," and although they wished to

return promptly to Fort Schuyler, Schuyler would try to persuade some of them to join Gates. On the 23rd, Dearborn would write that "about 100 Onyda Indians who Joined us the Next Day after the Battle [of the 19th], have Brought in more or Less Prisoners Every Day—" Colonel Jeduthan Baldwin gave the number as 112. Baldwin would also write on September 26 that "30 indians went of this day" and on the 27th that "the greatest part of the Indians went of home."

9. They were Christianized Mahican (or Mohican) Indians from Stockbridge, Massachusetts. They served as soldiers in the Massachusetts Continental line.

10. This was a detachment of one troop under a French officer, Captain Jean Louis de Vernejoux, who "ran away" on October 15. He was dismissed by Gates on the 20th, and replaced by Lieutenant (now Captain) Thomas Young Seymour.

3. ORGANIZATION OF THE ARMY UNDER THE COMMAND OF LIEUTENANT GENERAL JOHN BURGOYNE FROM SEPTEMBER 19 TO OCTOBER 7, 1777

John Burgoyne's headquarters staff
William Phillips' general staff

The Advanced Corps

(also called "Fraser's Corps")
commanded by Brigadier General Simon Fraser

British Light Infantry Battalion, Major Alexander Lindsay, 6th Earl of Balcarres [1]
24th Regiment of Foot, Major William Agnew
British Grenadier Battalion, Major John Dyke Acland [1]
Company of British Marksmen (Fraser's Rangers), Captain Alexander Fraser [2]
Company of Québec militia, Captain René Amable Boucher de Boucherville
Company of Montréal militia, Captain David Monin [3]
3rd Battalion, 7th Company Royal Artillery, with detachments from the
2nd Battalion, consisting of four 6-pounders, four 3-pounders, and two 5 1/2-inch howitzers, Captain Ellis Walker

The Right Wing of the Army

(also called the "British line" or "Hamilton's division")
commanded by Brigadier General James Hamilton

9th Regiment of Foot, Lieutenant Colonel John Hill
21st Regiment of Foot or Royal North British Fuziliers, Major George Forster
62nd Regiment of Foot, Lieutenant Colonel John Anstruther
20th Regiment of Foot, Lieutenant Colonel John Lind
4th Battalion, 3rd Company Royal Artillery, with a detachment from the 3rd Battalion, 8th Company, consisting of four 6-pounders, Captain Thomas Jones [4]

The Left Wing of the Army

(also called "von Riedesel's division")
commanded by Major General Friedrich Adolph, Baron von Riedesel

Baron von Riedesel's general staff
Brunswick Dragoon Regiment Prinz Ludwig, Captain Adolf von Schlagen-
teuffel [5]
Hesse-Hanau artillery, consisting of four 6-pounders, Captain Georg Päusch

1st German Brigade, commanded by Brigadier General Johann
Friedrich Specht
Brunswick Regiment von Riedesel, Lieutenant Colonel Ernst Ludwig
Wilhelm von Speth
Brunswick Regiment Specht, Major Carl Friedrich von Ehrenkrook
Brunswick Regiment von Rhetz, Major Balthasar Bogislaus von Lucke

2nd German Brigade, commanded by Brigadier General Wilhelm
Rudolph von Gall
Hesse-Hanau Regiment Erbprinz, Brigadier General Wilhelm Rudolph
von Gall

The Reserve Corps

(also called "Breymann's Corps")
commanded by Lieutenant Colonel Heinrich Christoph Breymann

Brunswick Grenadier Battalion, Lieutenant Colonel Heinrich Christoph
Breymann [6]
Brunswick Chasseur Battalion von Bärner, Major Ferdinand Albrecht
von Bärner
Hesse-Hanau artillery detachment of two 6-pounders, Bombardier
Conrad Wall

The Brigade of the Park of Artillery

commanded by Captains and Majors Griffith Williams and John Carter
Royal Irish Artillery detachment
33rd Regiment of Foot detachment, Lieutenant George Anson Nutt [7]

Right Division, commanded by 2nd Lieutenant Samuel Rimington
1st Battalion, Royal Artillery detachment of two 12-pounders and two
6-pounders

Center Division, commanded by Captain Lieutenant Thomas Blomefield
Royal Artillery brigade of two 24-pounders, two 8-inch howitzers, and two
5 1/2-inch howitzers served by detachments of Captain Griffith William's
Company of the 1st Battalion and Captain John Carter's Company of the 1st
Battalion

Left Division, commanded by Captain Lieutenant Thomas Hosmer
1st Battalion, Royal Artillery detachment of two 12-pounders and two
6-pounders

Loyalist Infantry

usually serving with the Advanced Corps

King's Loyal Americans (Jessup's Rangers), Lieutenant Colonel Ebenezer
Jessup [8]
Queen's Loyal Rangers (Peters' Corps), Lieutenant Colonel John Peters [9]
The Loyal Volunteers, Captain Samuel MacKay
"Voluntiers under the Command of Daniel McAlpin," Captain Daniel
McAlpin

"Major Campbell's department"

(also called the "Indian Department") commanded by Major John Campbell,
usually serving with the Advanced Corps

staff [10]
Iroquois Indians
Algonquian Indian warriors [11]

Attached to the Army

47th Regiment of Foot, Lieutenant Colonel Nicholas Sutherland [12]
1st Battalion, Royal Highland Emigrants detachment, Captain Lieutenant
George Lawes [13]
Royal Navy detachment, Lieutenant John Schank
Royal Engineers, Lieutenant William Twiss
commissary departments, Jonathan Clarke
Quartermaster Department, Captain John Money
Hospital Department, Acting Physician Vincent Wood
artificers
wagon-men, batteaux-men
sutlers [14]
camp followers [15]

Note: The battalion companies of the 53rd Regiment of Foot, 3rd Battalion,
8th Company of the Royal Artillery, the musketeer companies of the
Brunswick Regiment Prinz Friedrich, and a detachment of Canadians and
artificers were left behind at Fort Ticonderoga and Mount Independence.

1. Consisting of the respective companies from the 9th, 20th, 21st, 24th, 29th, 31st,
   34th, 47th, 53rd, and 62nd regiments.
2. This unit was also known as the "company of marksmen" under Captain Fraser

of the 34th Regiment. After it was destroyed at the First Battle of Bennington, the company was rebuilt on September 2 with 16 men and one NCO from each British regiment.

3. Killed on September 19 and replaced by Lieutenant Beaubien.
4. Killed on September 19 and replaced by 2nd Lieutenant James Hadden.
5. What remained of this regiment after most had been lost at Bennington on August 16 was one small squadron that finally received horses, with the men "shabbily mounted" on them.
6. This battalion consisted of the grenadier companies from the Brunswick regiments von Rhetz, Specht, von Riedesel, and Prinz Friedrich.
7. These were about 150 "additionals, recruits for the southern army." Most were destined for the 33rd, but some were meant for "other regiments." They were uniformed as infantry (according to their regiments), but were "attached to the service of the artillery," and served with the different detachments of artillery to fill them out. There is evidence that some of these recruits were intended for the undermanned 10th Regiment of Foot.
8. Recruited from Charlotte County, NY (now roughly Clinton, Essex, Franklin, Warren Counties, upper Washington County, and about 1/3 of upper Vermont).
9. Recruited from Albany County, NY (now roughly Albany, Columbia, Rensselaer, Saratoga, Schenectady, Schoharie Counties, much of Greene and Washington Counties, and Bennington County, Vermont).
10. The staff included Major John Campbell (who was superintendent of Indians in Canada), three lieutenants, one chaplain, "two volunteers," and seven servants.
11. Following the Battles of Bennington on August 16, "almost all the Savages [Indians] have gone home." The few warriors that remained would probably have been "Algonchins, Abenekies," and/or "Outawas."
12. The 47th Regiment sent two of its eight battalion companies to Fort George. They then moved to Diamond Island on Lake George for safety because of an expected American attack. The six companies that remained with Burgoyne were delegated to protect the batteaux.
13. This was a detachment of The Royal Highland Emigrants (designated the 84th Regiment of Foot in 1779), made up of six officers and men, attached to the artificers as engineers.
14. Sutlers were civilians who owned businesses and sold goods to the soldiers.
15. Two hundred fifteen British and 82 German women camp followers were present at the surrender.

4. A NOTE ON INFANTRY WEAPONS AND TACTICS

One of the most persistent traditions associated with the American Revolution is that a major factor in its success was the differences in the tactics of the adversaries. According to this interpretation the British and their German auxiliaries, captives of an outmoded tradition developed on Europe's open battlefields, marched into battle in close formation against skilled American sharpshooters who fought as individuals from the cover of trees and walls. Events at Lexington and Concord in 1775 and at Kings Mountain in 1780 seemed to lend support to this belief, but even in those engagements American marksmanship has been over-rated. Most of the battles of the war were fought by the soldiers of both armies according to standard European practice and with standard European weapons.

The basic infantry weapon of the 18th century was the flintlock musket, a smoothbore piece that fired a lead ball. The British "Brown Bess" would fire a ball approximately 3/4-inch in diameter (.75 caliber), while the favorite American musket, the French-made Charleville, would have the slightly smaller diameter of about 7/10 of an inch (.69 caliber). Because the ball fit so loosely in the barrel of these weapons, their accuracy was limited and their effectiveness depended upon the "linear tactics" of the time. A line of battle consisted of two or three ranks drawn up shoulder to shoulder or at an arms-length apart, with minimum depth between ranks. Another rank of "file closers" sometimes followed at about six paces to replace casualties. In the attack the men moved forward maintaining their alignment, aware that they were relatively safe until they were within about 100 yards of the enemy line. Fire discipline was important because it was desirable that soldiers not fire until they were about 50 yards from their opponents. In fact, the theory was that it was better to receive, not deliver, the first fire, to sustain the losses and fire when close enough to the foe that every shot found a mark.

Firing was by volley, not "at will." All loading and firing was done by command with little or no aiming in the modern sense. The volley was directed ahead or to the left or right oblique as commanded. The object was to lay down a curtain of fire, and rapidity was more highly prized than accuracy. A desired rate was one shot every fifteen seconds, a rate that would assure at least two volleys at an approaching enemy in a typical charge.

It is important to understand that the ranks of men were not normally in extended order. They formed a compact mass, presenting a good target for fire from another compact body of men at point blank range. As Harold L. Peterson, an authority on weapons and their effects, has observed, "Accuracy would have been superfluous in this type of warfare. Speed was everything. Speed for the defending force to pour as many bullets into the attacking force as possible; speed for the attacking force to close with its adversary before it had been too severely decimated to have sufficient strength to carry the position."

There were situations, even in Europe, in which a more accurate weapon was needed. Flankers, rangers, pickets, and small scouting parties where there was occasion for individual action required accurate marksmanship. It was for these men and in these circumstances that the rifle proved a valuable arm.

In contrast with the musket, the rifle was highly accurate. Rifling, or the spiral grooves in the bore of a firearm that cause a projectile to spin when fired, imparted greater stability to the bullet. When properly employed, as at Saratoga where Gates combined them with Dearborn's light infantry, the riflemen were invaluable for scouting, skirmishing, and sharpshooting. Except for these specialized operations they were of little military value. Like the muskets, rifles were single-shot weapons, but their slow rate of fire and their vulnerability to attack because they were rarely fitted with bayonets limited their usefulness.

Both armies at Saratoga had riflemen. The Americans had Colonel Daniel Morgan's battalion of riflemen. The British had German jägers (hunters) who performed the specialized functions for which they were equipped, while most of their comrades fought in line in compliance with standard practice. At

Saratoga, as elsewhere, the infantryman with a bayonet-bearing musket, capable of delivering a higher volume of fire than the rifle and with enough accuracy for the tactics of the period, was the man who won or lost the battle.

5. A NOTE ON INFANTRY ORGANIZATION

The regiment was the basic infantry unit of any army in the 18th century. A regiment, at full strength, consisted of about 600 officers and men. In the British army, the nominal or administrative commander was the colonel who contracted with the Crown to raise and/or run the regiment for a given sum of money. Except for the units that carried the title "Royal," the regiments were thus the property of the colonel, regulated by and under the ultimate control of the British government. The colonel of a regiment did not usually serve with his regiment, since he was a general in the army. For example, John Burgoyne was a major general in the British army, but he held the higher rank of lieutenant general "in America only." He was also the colonel of the 16th Queen's Light Dragoon Regiment, a unit that served with Sir William Howe in 1777. The active or personal commander of a regiment was the lieutenant colonel, who usually led the regiment in the field. James Hamilton was the lieutenant colonel of the 21st Regiment of Foot, but like Burgoyne, he too held a higher "local" rank, his being brigadier general. Since he now had an entire brigade of four regiments to command, the command of the 21st Regiment went to its third-in-command, a major. The standard British regiment had 10 companies of about 60 officers and men each, eight of which were called "battalion" or "hat" companies. The other two were the elite "flank companies," one company of grenadiers and one of light infantry. Grenadiers were the largest and toughest soldiers in the army, while the light infantrymen were the smallest and quickest. As they had since the beginning of the war at Lexington and Concord in 1775, the British would take all of the light infantry and grenadier companies from all of the regiments and place them into battalions of regimental size units. Therefore, the grenadier and light infantry battalions looked like regiments of grenadiers and light infantry.

The American regiments were modeled after the British, but the active command was exercised by the colonel until after January 1778, when the rank of "Lieutenant Colonel, Commandant" was created to facilitate the grade-for-grade exchange of regimental commanders who were prisoners of war. The number of companies and the strength of the American regiments varied from state to state and from time to time. In Gates' army in 1777, the size was eight companies to a regiment, and men joined a militia or Continental regiment depending on the county they lived in. Continental regiments were organized according to their home state, hence the "8th Massachusetts Regiment," while the militias were organized by counties, like "Colonel John McCrea's 13th Regiment, Albany County militia." There were few established light infantry companies in 1777, but many times, as in the case of Dearborn's light infantry battalion, men were drafted for the purpose. Some American regiments even had a grenadier company.

There were hundreds of separate German states (each virtually acting as its own country) in 1777, since Germany was not a single country until the latter part of the 19th century. The British government "leased" soldiers from six German states throughout the war, and two of them were represented in Burgoyne's army. Burgoyne's German troops were either from the army of Brunswick or Hesse-Hanau. Those from Hesse-Hanau were true "Hessians," while those from Brunswick were not. The German regiments were headed by a "chief," who, like a colonel in the British army, usually did not serve with his regiment. Baron von Riedesel was the chief of the Regiment von Riedesel, which he did personally lead to Freeman's farm toward the climax of the First Battle of Saratoga. Having a regiment's own chief or colonel leading it into battle was a source of inspiration for the troops of that regiment. These German regiments consisted of six companies each; five of which were "musketeers" and the sixth, a company of elite grenadiers. As in the British army, the Brunswick grenadier companies were all put into a single unit, forming the Brunswick grenadier battalion commanded by Lieutenant Colonel Heinrich Breymann. The Brunswick chasseur (a French word meaning "light infantry") Battalion von Bärner consisted of four companies of light infantrymen and one company of jägers.

6. A NOTE ON SOURCES

This narrative of the Saratoga campaign is based upon American, British, and German sources, most of which are in manuscript form. Those for the complex story of the British plans for 1777 are found in the Colonial Office Records, Series 5 and 42, Public Records Office, London; British Museum, Additional Manuscripts 34313, 37883, and 38209; Lt. Gen. John Burgoyne, *A State of the Expedition from Canada...*(London, 1780); the Lord George Germain and Henry Knox Papers in the William L. Clements Library, Ann Arbor, Mich.; Sir William Howe, *The Narrative of Lt. Gen. Sir William Howe in a Committee of the House of Commons...*(London, 1780); and Sir John Fortescue (ed.), The Correspondence of King George the Third from 1760 to December 1783 (6 vols., London, 1927-8).

Manuscript sources for the details of the campaign include the Philip Schuyler Papers in the New York Public Library; the Horatio Gates Papers in the New-York Historical Society, the Library of Congress, and the New York Public Library; the William Livingston and Benjamin Lincoln Papers and the Forbes Collection of New England Diaries in the Massachusetts Historical Society; the Henry Dearborn Papers in the New York Public Library; the Varick Papers in the New-York Historical Society; the Sir Henry Clinton Papers in the William L. Clements Library; the Ebenezer Stevens Papers in the New-York Historical Society; Briefschalten und Akten des General-leutenants Friedrich Adolf Riedesel, Freiherr zu Eisenbach; "Tagebuch Julius Fredrich Wasmus;" and "Fragment eines Tagebuch über die Braunschweig Truppen in Amerika, 1777." The last three items are in the Nieder-sachsisches Staatsarchiv, Wolfenbüttel, Germany.

Among the articles that provide useful details concerning the Saratoga campaign are two valuable studies by Jane Clark: "The Command of the Canadian Army for the Campaign of 1777," *Canadian Historical Review,* X (1929), and "The Responsibility for the Failure of the Burgoyne Campaign," *American Historical Review,* XXXV (1930); William B. Willcox, "Too Many Cooks: British Planning Before Saratoga," *Journal of British Studies,* II (1962-3); and John Luzader, "The Arnold-Gates Controversy," *West Virginia History,* January 1966.

Research has significantly changed the details and interpretation of Hoffman Nickerson's *The Turning Point of the American Revolution* (Boston, 1928), which was the definitive work on the subject for nearly 50 years. Troyer Anderson, *The Command of the Howe Brothers during the American Revolution* (New York, 1936); William B. Willcox, *Portrait of a General: Sir Henry Clinton in the War of Independence* (New York, 1964); William B. Willcox (ed.), *The American Rebellion: Sir Henry Clinton's Narrative of his Campaigns* (New Haven, 1954); Piers Mackesy, *The War for America 1775-1783* (Cambridge, Mass., 1964); John R. Alden, *The American Revolution 1775-1783* (New York, 1954); Willard M. Wallace, *Appeal to Arms* (New York, 1951); John C. Miller, *Triumph of Freedom* (New York, 1948); Don Higginbotham, *The War of American Independence* (New York, 1971); and Ira D. Gruber, *The Howe Brothers in the American Revolution* (New York, 1972); all contain valuable information on the campaign.

A limited number of studies of individuals and their careers contain valuable contributions to understanding the story of Saratoga. Among them are two works edited by George A. Billias: *George Washington's Generals* (New York, 1964) and *George Washington's Opponents: British Generals and Admirals in the American Revolution* (New York, 1969); Willard M. Wallace, *Traitorous Hero: The Life and Fortunes of Benedict Arnold* (New York, 1954); Don Higginbotham, *Daniel Morgan: Revolutionary Rifleman* (Chapel Hill, 1961); North Callahan, *Daniel Morgan: Ranger of the Revolution* (New York, 1961); Don R. Gerlach, *Philip Schuyler and the American Revolution in New York, 1733-1777* (Lincoln, Nebr., 1964); Martin H. Bush, *Revolutionary Enigma: A reappraisal of General Philip Schuyler of New York* (Port Washington, 1969); Samuel W. Patterson, *Horatio Gates: Defender of American Liberties* (New York, 1941); Gerald S. Brown, *The American Secretary: The Colonial Policy of Lord George Germain* (Ann Arbor, 1963); and Alan Valentine, *Lord George Germain* (New York, 1962).

Since publication of the 1975 first edition of this book, there have been many more scholarly works published, both primary and secondary sources, regarding the events of the Saratoga campaign of 1777. The most notable secondary works published have been John R. Elting's *The Battles of Saratoga* (Monmouth Beach, NJ, 1977) and Richard M. Ketchum's *Saratoga* (New York, 1997). *An Eyewitness Account of the American Revolution and New England Life* (Westport, CT, 1990) and *The Specht Journal* (Westport, CT, 1995), both translated by Helga Doblin and edited by Mary C. Lynn, have added tremendous detail and depth to the interpretations of the Saratoga campaign.

History of the Park

Ellen Hardin Walworth

From the time that the guns went silent at Saratoga, there has always been an interest in visiting the historic spot where the British suffered their major defeat at the hands of the rebellious American colonists. A first famous visitor to the battlegrounds was General George Washington who came to Saratoga as a guest of General Philip Schuyler in 1783. He was followed by future presidents Thomas Jefferson and James Madison and former President John Quincy Adams who visited in 1843 while staying at Saratoga Springs.

By the 1850's local interest in commemorating the Battles of Saratoga resulted in the formation of the Saratoga Monument Association. In 1877 this group of local, state, and national representatives took on the task of building the Saratoga Monument on the hilltop in Schuylerville where General Burgoyne's last camp was situated. Feeling that Americans should adopt the European tradition of touring historic battlefields, Ellen Hardin Walworth, one of the founders of the Daughters of the American Revolution and a committee member of the Saratoga Monument Association, arranged for the placement of granite tablets at significant locations on the battlefield in Stillwater. By 1893, there were a total of thirteen tablets celebrating the accomplishments of the American forces and their leaders in the decisive victory at Saratoga. The construction of the monument, after many delays caused by a lack of funding, was finally completed in 1887.

In the 1920's, with the Sesquicentennial of the battles approaching, the Saratoga Battlefield Association was formed to work towards preservation

Schuylerville, N.Y.,
Saratoga Monument-The finest of its kind in the World.

Saratoga Monument

ORIGINALLY ENVISIONED AS A
CENTENARY COMMEMORATION,
THE SARATOGA MONUMENT
FACED MANY FINANCIAL OBSTA-
CLES THAT PREVENTED ITS COM-
PLETION UNTIL 1888. THE STATE
OF NEW YORK ASSUMED ITS
OPERATION IN 1895; ITS FORMAL
DEDICATION TOOK PLACE IN
1912. THE MONUMENT BECAME
PART OF SARATOGA NATIONAL
HISTORICAL PARK IN 1980.

COURTESY OF LARRY GORDON

of the battlefield as a public park. The association was organized by prominent New York newspaper publisher Adolph Ochs, owner of *The New York Times*, and George Slingerland, mayor of Mechanicville, New York. These two men, along with local and nearby Rotary Clubs, undertook the task of acquiring the battlefield lands on Bemis Heights in Stillwater. In 1926 the state legislature passed the bill creating the Saratoga Battlefield, administered by the State of New York Conservation Commission. The battlefield's first full year of operation in 1927 was highlighted by a spectacular pageant held on the actual battlegrounds on October 8 involving a cast of thousands and viewed by over 150,000 spectators. Visitors to the new park were able to visit the 1777 home of John Neilson and the newly constructed "Blockhouse" museum.

With improved roads, and a staff of enthusiastic guides at the Blockhouse museum, the Saratoga Battlefield became a popular site to visit. Over the years, national figures such as Admiral Richard E. Byrd, many foreign dignitaries, and descendants of some of those who fought at Saratoga, visited this revered site. One particularly interested visitor was Franklin Delano Roosevelt, then governor of New York State. Roosevelt so enjoyed his visits to the battlefield that he frequently brought guests here, including five governors at one time when he was meeting with them to plan the annual National Conference of Governors.

Roosevelt's support for the battlefield continued after his election as president of the United States. It was under his administration that the National Park Service was given jurisdiction for many military parks, battlefields,

The Commemoration of 1927

TO MARK THE OCCASION OF ITS 150TH ANNIVERSARY,
THE SARATOGA BATTLEFIELD WAS THE SCENE OF A HUGE PAGEANT.
IT IS ESTIMATED THAT SOME 160,000 PEOPLE ATTENDED.

SARATOGA NATIONAL HISTORICAL PARK

military cemeteries, and historic sites. In 1938, Congress passed the authorizing legislation for Saratoga National Historical Park, officially making it a part of the National Park System. The president's influence extended to other decisions made at the park, including the siting of the visitor center and his intervention during World War II to keep the cannons surrendered by Burgoyne from being melted down for scrap metal.

The park's growth was slow during the Second World War, as the national work force and national budget were redirected to serving the needs of the armed forces and gas rationing severely limited visitation. Following the war, staffing levels returned to normal and many of the physical changes that are seen today were undertaken. A nine-mile loop tour road around the battlefield was begun. The visitor center was constructed on Fraser Hill as decided by President Roosevelt in 1940, and the general infrastructure of walks, trails, interpretive stops, and maintenance facilities were made. In preparation for the Bicentennial celebration of 1977, the National Park Service added an additional theater and museum exhibits to the visitor center.

In addition to the battlefield, Saratoga National Historical Park is entrusted with the care and maintenance of two additional sites—the General Schuyler House in Schuylerville, New York and the Saratoga Monument in nearby Victory, New York. The Schuyler House, one of the homes of Revolutionary War General Philip Schuyler, was added to the park in 1950 by donation. With the assistance of the Old Saratoga Historical Association, this historic house has been furnished with period pieces that illustrate the life of the Philip Schuyler family and tell the story of his personal and professional commitment during this trying period.

Schuyler House

The Saratoga Monument represents a significant period of American history in which the success and heroism of preceding generations was commemorated through memorials like the one at Bennington and the monument at Bunker Hill. Members of the Saratoga Monument Association conceived the idea of the monument in 1859 and persevered to see its cornerstone laid on the centennial in 1877 and final completion in 1887. Turned over to the State of New York in 1895, a formal dedication—which drew over 100,000 visitors—took place on the Sesquicentennial of the battles in 1912. In 1980, the State of New York transferred the monument to the National Park Service, which launched a major restoration and rehabilitation of the obelisk in 1999.

DECISION ON THE HUDSON

Associated Sites

BENNINGTON BATTLE MONUMENT
15 MONUMENT CIRCLE
BENNINGTON, VERMONT 05021
(802) 447-0550

Open daily from mid-April through October 31, 9:00 a.m. to 5:00 p.m.

The Battle of Bennington was actually fought on New York soil at Walloomscoick Creek, which followed the route used by Crown Forces to attain supplies stored at Bennington.

The 306-foot monument commemorates the battle and marks the location of the storehouses.

Approximate driving time from Saratoga NHP: 1 hour

BENNINGTON BATTLEFIELD
STATE HISTORIC SITE
R.D. #2 BOX 11
HOOSIC FALLS, NEW YORK
12090
(518) 279-1155

Open seasonally, 10 a.m. to dusk, weather permitting

In August 1777, Burgoyne's army was attempting to re-supply and make a final push for Albany. A column of some German auxiliaries and loyalists, along with a few British regulars and Native Americans was sent towards Bennington, Vermont. On August 16 at Walloomscoick Creek, militia under the command of John Stark and Seth Warner destroyed the column. A relief column sent from Burgoyne's army was also defeated and forced to retreat. Burgoyne suffered a shattering loss of some 900 troops during this engagement.

Approximate driving time from Saratoga NHP: 50 minutes

Fort Stanwix
National Monument
112 East Park Street
Rome, New York 13440
(315) 336-2090

Originally built in 1753 by the British, Fort Stanwix was renovated in 1776 by the Americans to defend the upper reaches of the Mohawk River Valley. Its successful defense against a besieging force under Colonel Barry St. Leger deprived Burgoyne of the support he needed during the campaign of 1777.

Approximate driving time from Saratoga NHP: 2 1/2 hours

Fort Ticonderoga
Fort Road Box 390
Ticonderoga, New York 12883
(518) 585-2821

Open mid May to mid October

Captured by the British from the French in the course of the Seven Years' War, the fort was taken by the rebellious Americans in 1775. During the Saratoga campaign, British General John Burgoyne's army seized the fort, and the limited American force retreated, escaping to the Vermont shore on July 6, 1777. A small garrison of British soldiers was left behind to hold Fort Ticonderoga. On September 18, 1777, American troops from Vermont attacked the fort, and although they were unsuccessful, the siege demonstrated the vulnerability of the garrison. When word of Burgoyne's surrender reached Ticonderoga, the garrison set fire to the fort and abandoned it.

Approximate driving time from Saratoga NHP: 1 1/2 to 2 hours

HUBBARDTON BATTLEFIELD STATE HISTORIC SITE HUBBARDTON, VERMONT (802) 273-2282

Open late May to mid October

After abandoning Ticonderoga and Mount Independence, the Americans retreated east and south through what is now Vermont. The British advance guard collided with the American rear guard on July 7, 1777. In a fierce fight, the Americans came close to turning the British flank. Defeat for the British was averted only by the timely arrival of a reinforcement of German troops.

Approximate driving time from Saratoga NHP: 1 1/2 to 2 hours

MOUNT INDEPENDENCE STATE HISTORIC SITE ORWELL, VERMONT (802) 948-2000

Open late May to mid October

Located on Lake Champlain directly across from Fort Ticonderoga, the fort at Mount Independence was designed to compensate for flaws in Ticonderoga's less than ideal southern location and poor condition. During Burgoyne's siege of Ticonderoga, Mount Independence proved to be an escape hatch for the American troops. British and German forces who remained at the garrison later burned and destroyed it after learning of Burgoyne's surrender at Saratoga.

Approximate driving time from Saratoga NHP: 1 1/2 to 2 hours

ASSOCIATED SITES

ORISKANY BATTLEFIELD
STATE HISTORIC SITE
7801 STATE ROUTE 69
ORISKANY, NEW YORK 13424
(315) 768-7224

While Fort Stanwix was under siege, an attempt was made by New York militia to relieve the garrison. Native Americans and loyalists from the force attacking Fort Stanwix ambushed the column of militia at Oriskany Creek, and in the terrible fighting that ensued, the militia suffered heavy casualties and barely held its ground.

Approximate driving time from Saratoga NHP: 2 hours

SCHUYLER MANSION
STATE HISTORIC SITE
32 CATHERINE STREET
ALBANY, NEW YORK 12202
(518) 434-0834

American Major General Philip Schuyler built his city home here in 1761. Following his surrender, General John Burgoyne was a "guest" of General Schuyler before traveling to join his defeated forces in Cambridge, Massachusetts.

Approximate driving time from Saratoga NHP: 1 hour

Fort Edward: Route 4, Fort Edward, New York. The fortifications that played an important role in the colonial wars have mostly disappeared under the village of Fort Edward. Once the largest British fort in North America, Fort Edward had fallen into disrepair by the time of Burgoyne's invasion.

Fort Anne: Route 4, Fort Ann, New York. This is the site of a battle on July 8, 1777. A bank in the form of a blockhouse stands near the site of the original 18th-century structure.

Fort Hardy (Field of Grounded Arms): Route 29, Schuylerville, New York. The site of a ruined fort from the French and Indian War (Seven Years' War). It was here that Burgoyne's defeated army lay down their arms on October 17, 1777.

Sword Surrender Site: Marked on US Route 4, one half-mile south of Schuylerville. As his troops laid down their arms, Burgoyne met Gates here and offered his sword as a token of surrender. The sword was returned, and the officers dined at Gates' headquarters.

ASSOCIATED SITES

Suggestions for Additional Reading

HISTORIES OF THE WAR FOR AMERICAN INDEPENDENCE

Rebels and Redcoats: The American Revolution Through the Eyes of Those Who Fought and Lived It by George F. Scheer and Hugh F. Rankin. Da Capo Press, New York, 1957.

Redcoats and Rebels: The American Revolution through British Eyes by Christopher Hibbert. Avon Books, New York, 1990.

The Black Presence in the Era of the American Revolution by Sidney Kaplan and Emma Nogrady Kaplan. University of Massachusetts Press, Amherst, 1989.

The War of American Independence: Military Attitudes, Policies and Practice 1763-1789 by Don Higginbotham. Northeastern University Press, Boston, 1983.

The Iroquois in the American Revolution by Barbara Graymont. Syracuse University Press, Syracuse, 1972.

SARATOGA CAMPAIGN

Saratoga: Turning Point of America's Revolutionary War by Richard M. Ketchum. Henry Holt, New York, 1997.

Escape In America: The British Convention Prisoners 1777-1783 by Richard Sampson. Picton Publishing, Chippingham (U.K.), 1995.

An Eyewitness Account of the American Revolution and New England Life: the Journal of J.F. Wasmus, German Company Surgeon, 1776-1783. Translated by Helga Doblin. Greenwood Press, New York, 1990.

Revolutionary War Journals of Henry Dearborn 1775-1783. Edited by Lloyd A. Brown and Howard H. Peckham. Da Capo Press, New York, 1971.

Baroness von Riedesel and the American Revolution: Journal and Correspondence of a Tour of Duty 1776-1783. Edited by Marvin L. Brown Jr. University of North Carolina Press, Chapel Hill, 1965.

SELECTED BIOGRAPHIES

The Generals of Saratoga: John Burgoyne & Horatio Gates by Max M. Mintz. Yale University Press, New Haven, 1990.

Benedict Arnold Revolutionary Hero by James Kirby Martin. New York University Press, New York, 1997.

Daniel Morgan Revolutionary Rifleman by Don Higginbotham. University of North Carolina Press, Chapel Hill, 1961.